"Somewhere to the eastward a wolf howled; lightly, questioningly. I knew the voice, for I had heard it many times before. It was George, sounding the wasteland for an echo from the missing members of his family. But for me it was a voice which spoke of the lost world which once was ours before we chose the alien role; a world which I had glimpsed and almost entered . . . only to be excluded, at the end, by my own self."

NEVER CRY WOLF
by
Farley Mowat

WALT DISNEY PICTURES PRESENTS

A CARROLL BALLARD FILM

NEVER CRY WOLF

Starring

CHARLES MARTIN SMITH and BRIAN DENNEHY

Executive Producer
RON MILLER

Screenplay by
**CURTIS HANSON and SAM HAMM and
RICHARD KLETTER**

Narration written by
**C.M. SMITH and EUGENE CORR and
CHRISTINA LUESCHER**

Based on the book by
FARLEY MOWAT

Associate Producer **WALKER STUART**

Produced by
**LEWIS ALLEN, JACK COUFFER and
JOSEPH STRICK**

Directed by
CARROLL BALLARD

Released by
BUENA VISTA DISTRIBUTION CO., INC.

NEVER CRY WOLF

by
Farley Mowat

BANTAM BOOKS
TORONTO · NEW YORK · LONDON · SYDNEY · AUCKLAND

For Angeline—the angel!

*This low-priced Bantam Book
has been completely reset in a type face
designed for easy reading, and was printed
from new plates. It contains the complete
text of the original hard-cover edition.*
NOT ONE WORD HAS BEEN OMITTED.

RL 7, IL age 12 and up

NEVER CRY WOLF

*A Bantam Book / published by arrangement with
Little, Brown and Company in association with
the Atlantic Monthly Press*

PRINTING HISTORY

*Little, Brown edition published September 1963
12 printings through July 1979*

Outdoor Life Book Club edition April 1964

Bantam edition / December 1979

2nd printing . . December 1979	6th printing . . November 1982
3rd printing . . . . . April 1980	7th printing . . . . January 1983
4th printing . . . . . . June 1981	8th printing . . . . . . July 1983
5th printing . . December 1981	9th printing . . . . January 1984

*All rights reserved.
Copyright © 1963, 1973 by Farley Mowat.
Cover copyright © 1983 by Walt Disney Productions.
This book may not be reproduced in whole or in part, by
mimeograph or any other means, without permission.
For information address: Little, Brown and Company,
34 Beacon Street, Boston, Massachusetts 02106.*

ISBN 0-553-23624-5

PRINTED IN THE UNITED STATES OF AMERICA

H   18 17 16 15 14 13

Preface

WHEN I BEGAN writing this book eleven years ago the wolf was cast in a rather minor role. My original plan was to write a satire about quite a different beast—that peculiar mutation of the human species known as the Bureaucrat. I intended the wolf to serve only as a foil for an exposition of *homo bureaucratis*—that aberrant product of our times who, cocooned in convention, witlessly wedded to the picayune, obsessed with obscurantism, and foundering in footling facts, nevertheless considers himself the only legitimate possessor of revealed truth and, consequently, the self-appointed arbiter of human affairs.

With malice aforethought, I deliberately set out to expose these new rulers of our world or, rather, to give them scope to expose themselves. But somewhere in the early part of the book I found myself losing interest in bureaucratic buffoonery. Without conscious volition I became increasingly engrossed with my secondary character, the wolf. Eventually the wolf took the book right out of my hands so that it became a plea for understanding, and preservation, of an extraordinarily highly evolved and attractive animal which was, and is, being harried into extinction by the murderous enmity and proclivities of man.

Never Cry Wolf was not kindly received by ordained authority. Because it is my practice never to allow facts to interfere with truth and because I believe that humour has its vital place even within the austere purlieus of science, many experts derided the book as a work of outright fiction, denying even that it was based on two summers and a winter during which I lived in the Arctic, closely associating with wolves. It gives me some small pleasure at this late date to note that almost every facet of wolf behaviour which I described has since been confirmed by "official" science. Unfortunately, my major thesis—that the wolf does not pose a threat to other wildlife, and is not a danger or a competitor of any consequence to man—remains largely unaccepted.

In 1973 several of the races of North American wolf—including the plains wolf, grey wolf and red wolf—are virtually extinct. In the whole of the continental United States (excluding Alaska) probably no more than 1,200 wolves survive. About 500 of these are in northern Minnesota, where they are partly protected by the Quetico National Park; but, in the autumn of 1972, the Minnesota State game authorities proposed a plan whereby 200 wolves a year would be destroyed by gun, snare, trap and poison—"until the wolf menace has been eliminated." In the vast expanse of forested but unsettled regions of Canada there were, until recently, about 15,000 timber wolves. However, the rapidly increasing use of light aircraft and, in particular, snowmobiles, has enabled massive numbers of hunters to penetrate these relatively inaccessible areas—with an inevitable reduction in the numbers of moose, deer, elk and other big-game animals. This has brought about the familiar cry from hunters, outfitters, guides, lodge owners and other financially interested parties: "Wolves are destroying the game—*the game that belongs to us!* We must act at once to destroy the wolf."

Who listens to this cry? Governments listen. Late in 1972, despite the contrary advice of his own biologists, the Quebec Minister of Fish and Game decreed a mass slaughter of wolves in the form of a contest open to hunters from Canada and the United States, with a goal of 5,000 dead wolves! Special prizes were to be awarded to the most successful hunters: the lower jawbone of a wolf encased in a block of clear plastic, suitably inscribed as an enduring testament to the skill, courage and hardihood of the human killer.

There is, however, a small ray of hope for the wolves. During the past decade a number of ordinary people have banded together to counter the anti-wolf pressure groups. They have had some successes. Largely due to the persistent efforts of the mere handful of people who constitute the Ontario Wolf League* (supported by some of the new biologists who are more interested in the study of living animals than in the study of the dead), the Ontario government recently revoked the iniquitous provincial bounty on wolves. In similar fashion, the group known as Canadian and American Wolf Defenders† may, just possibly, have forced the Minnesota government to drop its plans to exterminate the wolf in that State.

When this book was published in the Soviet Union the translators had a little trouble with the title. The version they finally came up with was: *Wolves, Please Don't Cry.* I hope it is a portent of things to come. It may be that there is still time to prevent mankind from committing yet another in the long list of his crimes against nature—the elimination from this planet of a fellow creature which has at least an equal *right* to life. If we can indeed save the

---

*Ontario Wolf League, P.O. Box 177, Postal Station "S," Toronto 382, Ontario.

†Canadian and American Wolf Defenders, 68 Panetta Road, Carmel Valley, California 93924, U.S.A.

wolf it will, in some small measure, be a rejection of the strictly human crime . . . of biocide.

Farley Mowat
Isles de la Madeleine
1973

Contents

1

The Lupine Project

IT IS A long way in time and space from the bathroom of my Grandmother Mowat's house in Oakville, Ontario, to the bottom of a wolf den in the Barren Lands of central Keewatin, and I have no intention of retracing the entire road which lies between. Nevertheless, there must be a beginning to any tale; and the story of my sojourn amongst the wolves begins properly in Granny's bathroom.

When I was five years old I had still not given any indication—as most gifted children do well before that age—of where my future lay. Perhaps because they were disappointed by my failure to declare myself, my parents took me to Oakville and abandoned me to the care of my grandparents while they went off on a holiday.

The Oakville house—"Greenhedges" it was called —was a singularly genteel establishment, and I did not feel at home there. My cousin, who was resident in Greenhedges and was some years older than myself, had already found his métier, which lay in the military field, and had amassed a formidable army of lead soldiers with which he was single-mindedly preparing himself to become a second Wellington. My loutish inability to play Napoleon exasperated him so much that he refused to have anything to do with me except under the most formal circumstances.

Grandmother, an aristocratic lady of Welsh descent who had never forgiven her husband for having been a retail hardware merchant, tolerated me but terrified me too. She terrified most people, including Grandfather, who had long since sought surcease in assumed deafness. He used to while away the days as calm and unruffled as Buddha, ensconced in a great leather chair and apparently oblivious to the storms which swirled through the corridors of Greenhedges. And yet I know for a fact that he could hear the word "whiskey" if it was whispered in a room three stories removed from where he sat.

Because there were no soulmates for me at Greenhedges, I took to roaming about by myself, resolutely eschewing the expenditure of energy on anything even remotely useful; and thereby, if anyone had had the sense to see it, giving a perfectly clear indication of the pattern of my future.

One hot summer day I was meandering aimlessly beside a little local creek when I came upon a stagnant pool. In the bottom, and only just covered with greeen scum, three catfish lay gasping out their lives. They interested me. I dragged them up on the bank with a stick and waited expectantly for them to die; but this they refused to do. Just when I was convinced that they were quite dead, they would open their broad ugly jaws and give another gasp. I was so impressed by their stubborn refusal to accept their fate that I found a tin can, put them in it along with some scum, and took them home.

I had begun to like them, in an abstract sort of way, and wished to know them better. But the problem of where to keep them while our acquaintanceship ripened was a major one. There were no washtubs in Greenhedges. There *was* a bathtub, but the stopper did not fit and consequently it would not hold water for more than a few minutes. By bedtime I had still not resolved the problem and, since I felt that even these doughty fish could hardly survive an entire night in the tin can, I was driven to the admittedly desperate expedient of finding temporary lodgings for them in the bowl of Granny's old-fashioned toilet.

I was too young at the time to appreciate the special problems which old age brings in its train. It was one of these problems which was directly responsible for the dramatic and unexpected encounter which took place between my grandmother and the catfish during the small hours of the ensuing night.

It was a traumatic experience for Granny, and for me, and probably for the catfish too. Throughout the rest of her life Granny refused to eat fish of any kind, and always carried a high-powered flashlight with her during her nocturnal peregrinations. I cannot be as certain about the effect on the catfish, for my unfeeling cousin—once the hooferaw had died down a little—callously flushed the toilet. As for myself, the effect was to engender in me a lasting affinity for the lesser beasts of the animal kingdom. In a word, the affair of the catfish marked the beginning of my career, first as a naturalist, and later as a biologist. I had started on my way to the wolf den.

My infatuation with the study of animate nature grew rapidly into a full-fledged love affair. I found that even the human beings with whom the study brought me into contact could be fascinating too. My first mentor was a middle-aged Scotsman who gained his livelihood delivering ice, but who was in fact an ardent amateur mammalogist. At a tender age he had developed mange, or leprosy, or some other such infantile disease, and had lost all his hair, never to recover it—a tragedy which may have had a bearing on the fact that, when I knew him, he had already devoted fifteen years of his life to a study of the relationship between summer molt and incipient narcissism in pocket gophers. This man had become so intimate with gophers that he could charm them with sibilant whistles until they would emerge from their underground retreats and passively allow him to examine the hair on their backs.

Nor were the professional biologists with whom I later came into contact one whit less interesting. When I was eighteen I spent a summer doing field work in the company of another mammalogist, seventy years of age, who was replete with degrees and whose towering stature in the world of science had been earned largely by an exhaustive study of uterine scars in shrews. This man, a revered professor at a large American university, knew more about the uteri of shrews than any other man has ever known. Furthermore he could talk about his subject with real enthusiasm. Death will find me long before I tire of contemplating an evening spent in his company during which he enthralled a mixed audience consisting of a fur trader, a Cree Indian matron, and an Anglican missionary, with an hour-long monologue on sexual aberrations in female pygmy shrews. (The trader misconstrued the tenor of the discourse; but the missionary, inured by years of humorless dissertations, soon put him right.)

My early years as a naturalist were free and fascinating, but as I entered manhood and found that my avocation must now become my vocation, the walls began to close in. The happy days of the universal scholar who was able to take a keen interest in all phases of natural history were at an end, and I was forced to recognize the unpalatable necessity of specializing, if I was to succeed as a professional biologist. Nevertheless, as I began my academic training at the university, I found it difficult to choose the narrow path.

For a time I debated whether or not to follow the lead of a friend of mine who was specializing in scatology—the study of the excretory droppings of animals—and who later became a high-ranking scatologist with the United States Biological Survey. But although I found the subject mildly interesting, it failed to rouse my enthusiasm to the pitch where I could wish to make it my lifework. Besides, the field was overcrowded.

My personal predilections lay towards studies of living animals in their own habitat. Being a literal fellow, I took the word *biology*—which means the study of life—at its face value. I was sorely puzzled by the paradox that many of my contemporaries tended to shy as far away from living things as they could get, and chose to restrict themselves instead to the aseptic atmosphere of laboratories where they used dead—often very dead—animal material as their subject matter. In fact, during my time at the university it was becoming unfashionable to have *anything* to do with animals, even dead ones. The new biologists were concentrating on statistical and analytical research, whereby the raw material of life became no more than fodder for the nourishment of calculating machines.

My inability to adjust to the new trends had an adverse effect upon my professional expectations. While my fellow students were already establishing themselves in various esoteric specialties, most of which they invented for themselves on the theory that if you are the *only* specialist in a given field you need fear no competition, I was still unable to deflect my interests from the general to the particular. As graduation approached I found that the majority of my contemporaries were assured of excellent research jobs while I seemed to have nothing particular to offer in the biological marketplace. It was, therefore, inevitable that I should end up working for the Government.

The die was cast one winter's day when I received a summons from the Dominion Wildlife Service informing me that I had been hired at the munificent salary of one hundred and twenty dollars a month, and that I "would" report to Ottawa at once.

I obeyed this peremptory order with hardly more than a twitch of subdued rebelliousness, for if I had learned anything during my years at the university it was that the scientific hierarchy requires a high standard of obedience, if not subservience, from its acolytes.

Two days later I arrived in the windswept, gray-souled capital of Canada and found my way into the dingy labyrinth which housed the Wildlife Service. Here I presented myself to the Chief Mammalogist, whom I had known as a school chum in more care-free days. But alas, he had now metamorphosed into a full-blown scientist, and was so shrouded in professional dignity that it was all I could do to refrain from making him a profound obeisance.

Through the next several days I was subjected to something called "orientation"—a process which, so far as I could see, was designed to reduce me to a malleable state of hopeless depression. At any rate, the legions of Dantesque bureaucrats whom I visited in their gloomy, Formalin-smelling dens, where they spent interminable hours compiling dreary data or originating meaningless memos, did nothing to rouse in me much devotion to my new employment. The only thing I actually *learned* during this period was that, by comparison with the bureaucratic hierarchy in Ottawa, the scientific hierarchy was a brotherhood of anarchy.

This was driven home one memorable day when, having at last been certified as fit for inspection, I was paraded into the office of the Deputy Minister, where I so far forgot myself as to address him as "Mister." My escort of the moment, all white-faced and trembling, immediately rushed me out of the Presence and took me by devious ways to the men's washroom. Having first knelt down and peered under

the doors of all the cubicles to make absolutely
certain we were alone and could not be overheard,
he explained in an agonized whisper that I must
never, on pain of banishment, address the Deputy
as anything but "Chief," or, barring that, by his Boer
War title of "Colonel."

Military titles were *de rigeur*. All memos were
signed Captain-this or Lieutenant-that if they
originated from the lower echelons; or Colonel-this
and Brigadier-that if they came down from on high.
Those members of the staff who had not had the
opportunity to acquire even quasi-military status
were reduced to the expedient of inventing suitable
ranks—field ranks if they were senior men, and
subaltern ranks for the juniors. Not everyone took
this matter with due solemnity, and I met one new
employee in the fishery section who distinguished himself briefly by sending a memo up to the Chief
signed "J. Smith, Acting Lance-Corporal." A week
later this foolhardy youth was on his way to the
northernmost tip of Ellesmere Island, there to spend
his exile living in an igloo while studying the life
history of the nine-spined stickleback.

Levity was not looked upon with favor anywhere
in those austere offices, as I discovered for myself
while attending a conference concerning my first
assignment.

A tentative list of the material requirements for this
assignment lay on the conference table, surrounded
by many grave countenances. It was a formidable
document, made out in quintuplicate—as was the
official rule—and imposingly headed:

DESIDERATA FOR THE LUPINE PROJECT

Having already been unnerved by the gravity of
the gathering, I lost my head completely when the

assembly began to consider the twelfth item listed
in this horrendous document:

Paper, toilet, Government standard: 12 rolls.

An austere suggestion by the representative of the
Finance Department that, in the interest of economy,
the quantity of this item might be reduced, providing
the field party (which was me) exercised all due
restraint, sent me into an hysterical spasm of giggling.
I mastered myself almost instantly, but it was too
late. The two most senior men, both "majors," rose
to their feet, bowed coldly, and left the room without
a word.

The Ottawa ordeal drew toward its end; but the
climax was still to come. One early spring morning
I was called to the office of the senior officer who
was my direct chief, for a final interview before departing "into the field."

My chief sat behind a massive desk whose dusty
surface was littered with yellowing groundhog skulls
(he had been studying rates of tooth decay in groundhogs ever since he joined the Department in 1897).
At his back hung the frowning, bearded portrait of
an extinct mammalogist who glared balefully down
upon me. The smell of Formalin swirled about like
the fetid breath of an undertaker's back parlor.

After a long silence, during which he toyed por-
tentously with some of his skulls, my chief began his
briefing. There was a solemnity about the occasion
which would have done justice to the briefing of a
special agent about to be entrusted with the assassi-
nation of a Head of State.

"As you are aware, Lieutenant Mowat," my chief
began, "the *Canis lupus* problem has become one of
national importance. Within this past year alone
this Department has received no less than thirty-
seven memoranda from Members of the House of
Commons, all expressing the deep concern of their

constituents that we ought to do something about the
wolf. Most of the complaints have come from such
civic-minded and disinterested groups as various
Fish and Game clubs, while members of the business
community—in particular the manufacturers of some
well-known brands of ammunition—have lent their
weight to the support of these legitimate grievances
of the voting public of this Great Dominion, because
their grievance is the complaint that the wolves are
killing all the deer, and more and more of our fellow
citizens are coming back from more and more hunts
with less and less deer.

"As you may possibly have heard, my predecessor
supplied the Minister with an explanation of this
situation in which it was his contention that there
were fewer deer because the hunters had increased
to the point where they outnumbered the deer about
five to one. The Minister, in all good faith, read this
fallacious statement in the House of Commons, and
he was promptly shouted down by Members howling
'Liar!' and 'Wolf-lover!'

"Three days later my predecessor retired to civil-
ian life, and the Minister issued a press statement:
'The Department of Mines and Resources is
determined to do everything in its power to curb the
carnage being wreaked upon the deer population by
hordes of wolves. A full-scale investigation of this
vital problem, employing the full resources of the
Department, is to be launched at once. The people
of this country can rest assured that the Government
of which I have the honor to be a member will
leave no stone unturned to put an end to this intolerable situation.'"

At this juncture my chief seized a particularly
robust groundhog skull and began rhythmically
clacking its jaws together as if to emphasize his final
words:

"You, Lieutenant Mowat, have been chosen for this
great task! It only remains for you to go out into the

field at once and tackle this work in a manner worthy of the great traditions of this Department. The wolf, Lieutenant Mowat, is now *your* problem!"

Somehow I staggered to my feet, and with an involuntary motion brought my right hand up in a smart salute before fleeing from the room.

I fled from Ottawa too . . . that self-same night, aboard a Canadian Air Force transport plane. My immediate destination was Churchill, on the western shore of Hudson Bay; but beyond that, somewhere in the desolate wastes of the subarctic Barren Lands, lay my ultimate objective—the wolf himself.

2

Wolf Juice

THE AIR FORCE transport was a twin-engined plane
capable of carrying thirty passengers, but by the time
all my "desiderata" were aboard there was barely
room left for the crew and me. The pilot, an amiable
flight lieutenant wearing a handlebar mustache,
watched the load going aboard with honest bewilderment writ large across his brow. His only information
about me was that I was some sort of Government
man going on a special mission to the Arctic. His
expression grew increasingly quizzical as we swung
three great bundles of clanking wolf traps into the
cabin, following these with the midsection of a col-
lapsible canoe which looked like nothing so much as
a bathtub without ends. True to Departmental prece-
dent, the bow and stern sections of this canoe had been
shipped to another biologist who was studying rattle-
snakes in the south Saskatchewan desert.

My armament was loaded aboard next. It consisted
of two rifles, a revolver complete with holster and
cartridge belt, two shotguns, and a case of tear-gas
grenades with which I was expected to persuade
reluctant wolves to leave their dens so that they
could be shot. There were also two large smoke generators prominently labeled DANGER, to be used for
signaling to aircraft in case I got lost or—perhaps—in
case the wolves closed in. A case of "wolf getters"—
fiendish devices which fire a charge of potassium
cyanide into the mouth of any animal which inves-
tigates them—completed my arsenal.

My scientific gear followed, including two five-gallon cans at the sight of which the pilot's eyebrows shot right up under his cap. They were marked: *100% Grain Alcohol for the Preservation of Specimen Stomachs.*

Tents, camp stoves, sleeping bags, and a bundle of seven axes (to this day I do not know why *seven*, for I was going to a treeless land where even one would have been superfluous), skis, snowshoes, dog harness, a radio transceiver and innumerable boxes and bales whose contents were as inscrutable to me as to the pilot, followed in due course.

When everything was in and securely roped down, the pilot, copilot and I crawled over the mass of gear and wedged ourselves into the cockpit. The pilot, having been thoroughly trained in the demands of military security, mastered his rampant curiosity as to the nature and purpose of my bizarre outfit and contented himself with the gloomy comment that he "doubted if the old crate could get airborne, with all that lot aboard." Secretly I doubted it too, but although the plane rattled and groaned dismally, she managed to take off.

The flight north was long and uneventful, except that we lost one engine over James Bay and had to complete the journey at an altitude of five hundred feet through rather dense fog. This minor contretemps temporarily took the pilot's mind off the problem of who and what I was; but once we had landed in Churchill he was unable to contain his curiosity any longer.

"I know it's none of my damn' business," he began apologetically as we walked toward one of the hangars, "but for heaven's sake, chum, what's up?"

"Oh," I replied cheerfully, "I'm going off to spend a year or two living with a bunch of wolves, that's all."

The pilot grimaced as if he were a small boy who had been justly rebuked for an impertinence.

"Sorry," he mumbled contritely. "Never should have asked."

That pilot was not the only one who was curious. When I began trying to make arrangements in Churchill for a commercial bush-plane to fly me on into the interior, my innocent explanation of my purpose, together with the honest admission that I hadn't the slightest idea where, in the almost untraveled wilderness, I wanted to be set down, drew either hostile stares of disbelief or conspiratorial winks. However, I was not deliberately trying to be evasive; I was only trying to follow the operation order which had been laid down for me in Ottawa:

Para. 3
  Sec. (C)
    Subpara. (iii)

You will, immediately upon reaching Churchill, proceed by chartered air transport in a suitable direction for the requisite distance and thereupon establish a Base at a point where it has been ascertained there is an adequate wolf population and where conditions generally are optimal to the furtherance of your operations. . . .

Although these instructions were firm in tone, they were rather lacking in specific direction, and I suppose it was only natural that half the population of Churchill should have concluded I was a member of a high-grade gang of gold-ore thieves attempting to make contact with my fellow conspirators; while the other half thought I was a prospector with knowledge of a secret mine somewhere in the vast interior Barrens. Later on, both these theories were discarded in favor of a vastly more intriguing one. When I eventually re-established contact with Churchill after many months of absence, it was to discover that the nature of my "real" mission had become public property: I had, so I then learned, actually spent the intervening months floating around the North Pole on an ice floe, keeping tabs on the activities of a crowd of Russians who were drifting about on *their* ice floe. My two cans of grain alcohol were believed to have been vodka, with which to loosen the tongues of the parched Russians in order to pry out their innermost secrets.

I became something of a hero after that story gained acceptance; but as I walked the bleak and snow-filled streets of Churchill shortly after my arrival there, trying to find a bush pilot to fly me to an unknown destination, I had not yet achieved hero status, and most of the people I spoke to were unhelpful.

After some delay I located the pilot of an ancient Fairchild ski-plane who made his precarious living flying Barren Land trappers to their remote cabins. When I put my problem to him he was roused to exasperation.

"Listen, Mac!" he cried. "Only nuts hire planes to go somewhere they don't know where; and only nuts'd expect a guy to swallow a yarn about goin' off to keep house with a bunch of wolves. You go find yourself another plane jockey, see? I'm too busy to play games."

As it happened there *were* no other plane jockeys in the dismal shacktown of Churchill at that time, although, shortly before my arrival, there had been three. One of them had made a miscalculation while attempting to land on the pack ice of Hudson Bay in order to shoot a polar bear—and the bear had been the sole survivor of the attempt. The second was away in Winnipeg trying to float a loan with which to purchase a new plane after the wing of his previous aircraft had come unstuck during a takeoff. The third was, of course, the one who was too busy to play games.

Since I could not adhere strictly to my original orders, I did what I thought was the next best thing, and radioed Ottawa for new instructions. The reply came back promptly, six days later:

> UNABLE UNDERSTAND YOUR DIFFICULTIES STOP
> YOUR INSTRUCTIONS ARE PERFECTLY CLEAR STOP IF
> CAREFULLY FOLLOWED NO DIFFICULTIES SHOULD DE-
> VELOP STOP WHEN SENDING COMMERCIAL RADIO
> MESSAGES TO THIS DEPARTMENT YOU ARE INSTRUCTED
> TO RESTRICT YOURSELF TO MATTERS OF UTMOST IM-
> PORTANCE AND UNDER NO CIRCUMSTANCES REPEAT
> UNDER NO CIRCUMSTANCES SHOULD THESE MESSAGES
> BE LONGER THAN TEN WORDS STOP EXPECT INTERIM
> PROGRESS REPORT WITHIN TWO WEEKS BY WHICH
> TIME IT IS ANTICIPATED YOU SHOULD HAVE
> ESTABLISHED CLOSE CONTACT WITH CANIS LUPUS
> STOP RADIO MESSAGES AT DEPARTMENTAL EXPENSE
> SHOULD BE RESTRICTED TO TEN WORDS AND IM-
> PORTANT MATTERS ONLY AND KEPT AS BRIEF AS
> POSSIBLE STOP WHAT DO YOU MEAN YOU HAVE ONLY
> HALF A CANOE STOP THE COST OF YOUR RADIOGRAM
> IS BEING DEBITED AGAINST YOUR SALARY
>
> CHIEF PREDATION CONTROL DIVISION

There was clearly nothing for it but to await the problematical return of the pilot who had gone to Winnipeg. Meanwhile I stayed at the local hotel, a creaking barn through whose gaping walls a fine drift of snow used to whirl and settle on a windy day. There was no other kind of day in Churchill.

Nevertheless I was not idle. Churchill was then full of missionaries, prostitutes, mounted policemen, rum-runners, trappers, fur smugglers, ordinary fur traders and other interesting characters, all of whom, so it developed, were authorities on wolves. One by one I sought them out and studiously copied down what they had to tell me. From these sources I received some fascinating information, most of which had never previously been recorded in the scientific literature. I discovered that, although wolves reputedly devour several hundred people in the Arctic Zone every year, they will always refrain from attacking a pregnant Eskimo. (The missionary who provided me with this remarkable data was convinced that the wolfish antipathy toward pregnant flesh encouraged a high birthrate among the Eskimos and a consequent lamentable concern with reproductive rather than spiritual matters.) I was told that every four years wolves are subject to a peculiar disease which causes them to shed their entire skins—and during the period when they are running about naked they are so modest they will curl up in a ball if closely approached. The trappers whom I interviewed informed me that wolves were rapidly destroying the caribou herds; that each wolf killed thousands of caribou a year just out of blood-lust, while no trapper would think of shooting a caribou except under the most severe provocation. One of the working ladies of the settlement added the odd bit of information that since the establishment there of an American Air Base the wolf population had increased out of all bounds, and the only thing to do when bitten by one was to bite him right back.

Quite early in my inquiry I was asked by an old trapper if, since I was a wolf enthusiast, I would like some wolf-juice. I said I did not think I would relish the drink, but since I *was* a scientist and anything to do with wolves was grist to my mill, I was willing to have a go. The old man thereupon led me off to Churchill's only beer parlor (a place I would normally have avoided) and introduced me to wolf-juice: a mixture which consisted of something called Moose Brand Beer liberally adulterated with antifreeze alcohol obtained from the soldiers at the Air Base.

Shortly after my baptism of wolf-juice I submitted my first progress report. It was in longhand and (perhaps fortunately for my continuing employment with the Department) proved completely indecipherable. No one in Ottawa could read a word of it; from which fact it was assumed that the report must be tremendously erudite. This report is, I believe, still on file with the Department, and is still consulted by Government specialists requiring expert data about wolves. As recently as last month I met a biologist who had seen it and who assured me that it was considered by many authorities to be the final word on *Canis lupus*.

Not only did I unearth many fascinating facts about wolves during my enforced stay in Churchill but I also made an independent discovery, possibly of even greater importance. I discovered that when the laboratory alcohol with which I had been supplied, was mixed sparingly with Moose Brand Beer a variety of wolf-juice resulted which was positively ambrosial. Thoughtfully I added fifteen cases of Moose Brand to my "desiderata." I also purchased several gallons of formaldehyde—which, as any undertaker will confirm, is at least as good a preservative of dead animal tissue as is grain alcohol.

3

Happy Landings

MY ENFORCED STAY in Churchill came to an end during the last week in May. For three days there had been a howling blizzard; then, during the third day, with visibility reduced to zero by blinding snow squalls, an aircraft came over the hotel at nought feet and with an expiring stutter flopped down on the ice of a nearby pond. The wind nearly blew it away again and would have done so had not several of us rushed out of the beer parlor and caught hold of its wings.

This plane was an outrageously decrepit bi-motor built in 1938 as a military training aircraft. It had been discarded after long years of service, only to be resuscitated by a lanky, hollow-eyed ex-R. A. F. pilot who had delusions about starting his own airline in the Canadian North. He descended from the creaky machine as we struggled to keep it on the ground and, having untwined a yard-long cerise silk scarf from around his face, introduced himself. He had come, he said, from Yellowknife, some seven hundred miles to the northwest, and his destination was The Pas . . . . . "was this The Pas?" Gently we informed him that The Pas lay some four hundred miles to the southwest. This news did not seem to dismay him. "Ah, well, any old port in a storm," he said gaily, and having been joined by his sluggish mechanic he accompanied us back to the beer parlor.

Here, somewhat later in the day, I found myself confessing my difficulty to him.

"No problem," he said after he had heard me out in attentive silence. "Gas up the old kite tomorrow and take you anywhere. Fly northwest—best course for us. Can't trust compass on any other course. Fly nice and low. Find lots of wolves; then put you down, and Happy Landings!"

He was almost as good as his word, although the next three days proved inauspicious for the flight—first because of a cloud cover at ground level, and secondly because the ski-equipped plane had developed a severe limp as a result of the collapse of one of the hydraulic cylinders of the landing gear. There was nothing we could do about the weather, but the plane's engineer discovered it was possible to restore the hydraulic cylinder to duty by filling it with seal-oil. It still leaked, but the plane would remain upright for as long as twenty minutes at a time before keeling over on its side again like a dying duck.

On the morning of the fourth day we prepared to depart. Because the plane could carry only a small load, I was forced to jettison some of my "desiderata," including the useless canoe-cum-bathtub. I was able, however, to trade a gallon of alcohol for a seventeen-foot canvas-covered canoe in fair condition, and this—so the pilot assured me—we could carry with us lashed under the belly of the aircraft.

At this point I played a somewhat underhanded trick on this obliging fellow. My Moose Brand had been amongst the gear set aside as nonessential; but one evening, by flashlight, I discovered that the whole fifteen cases would fit nicely into the canoe which, when tied tightly up against the plane's belly, betrayed nothing of the vital cargo which it carried.

It was a beautiful day when we departed. The wind had sunk to about forty miles an hour from the east, and there was no snow falling as we took off through a black sea fog, promptly lost sight of Churchill, and circled into the northwest.

Actually it was not quite that easy. A brief thaw the previous day had allowed the plane's skis to sink into an inch or two of slush, where they had frozen solid to the underlying ice. Our first attempt at a takeoff was anticlimatic, for even with both engines bellowing in an agonized manner the plane refused to budge. This recalcitrant behavior seemed to mystify pilot and engineer alike, and it was not until some of the gentlemen from the beer parlor ran out, and stood shouting soundlessly against the roar and pointing at our skis, that we began to comprehend the nature of our dilemma. Helped by these willing fellows we eventually managed to rock the plane loose, but not before the weak cylinder had collapsed again, thereby occasioning a further delay while another shot of seal-oil was administered.

Free at last to begin our takeoff run, the aircraft confounded its pilot by resolutely refusing to become airborne. We went skittering down the small lake with throttles wide open, but remained icebound. At the last minute the pilot shoved the rudder hard over and we skidded around sending up a great gout of snow, very nearly capsizing us before we could return in some embarrassment to our starting point.

"Bloody strange," said the pilot. "She *ought* to take off, you know, *really* ought. Ah well, better unload these drums of reserve petrol and give her a bit more lift."

The "reserve" drums had been taken aboard for his return trip to Churchill and I thought it rather reckless of him to jettison them, but since he was in command I let him have his way.

Without the surplus gas we managed on our next attempt (and after once again pumping up that cylinder) to get the aircraft into her own element. She did not seem particularly happy to be there.

She steadfastly refused to climb above three hundred feet, and the revolution indicators for both engines remained fixed at about three quarters of their proper readings.

"No need to go high anyway," the pilot bellowed cheerfully in my ear. "Wouldn't see the wolves. Keep your eyes skinned now. . . ."

Craning my head to peer out of the cracked and mazed plexiglass window I skinned my eyes as best I could, but with little result. We were flying in the midst of an opaque gray cloud and frequently I was unable even to see the wingtip. I saw no wolves, nor any sign of wolves.

We droned on for nearly three hours, during which we might as well have been submerged in a barrel of molasses for all we could see of the world below. At the end of this time the pilot put the aircraft into a steep dive and at the same time yelled to me:

"Going down now! Only enough petrol to get home. Good wolf country around here, though. Best kind of wolves!"

We emerged under the cloud at an altitude of something over thirty feet, and discovered we were flying up a mile-wide valley between high rocky hills, and over the surface of a frozen lake. Without an instant's hesitation the pilot landed, and whatever I may have thought of his aeronautical ability previously, I was suitably impressed with this particular maneuver, for he landed on our one good ski. Not until the aircraft had lost almost all speed did he allow her to settle slowly over on her weak starboard leg.

The pilot did not cut the engines.

"This is it, chum," he said merrily. "Out you go now. Got to be quick. Be dark before we raise Churchill."

The lethargic mechanic sprang to life and, in mere

moments, so it seemed to me, my mountain of supplies was on the ice, the canoe had been cut loose, and the landing-gear cylinder had once again been pumped back to the vertical.

After a glance at the contents of the canoe, the pilot bent a sorrowful look upon me.

"Not quite cricket, eh?" he asked. "Ah well, suppose you'll need it. Cheery-bob. Come back for you in the fall sometime if the old kite hasn't pranged. Not to worry, though. Sure to be lots of Eskimos around. They'll take you back to Churchill any time at all."

"Thanks," I said meekly. "But just for my records, do you mind telling me where I am?"

"Sorry about that. Don't quite know myself. Say about three hundred miles northwest of Churchill? Close enough. No maps of this country anyway. . . . Toodle-oo."

The cabin door slammed shut. The engines did their best to roar in the prescribed manner, and the plane went bumping across the pressure ridges, lifted unwillingly, and vanished into the overcast.

I had arrived safely at my base.

4

When Is a Wolf Not a Wolf?

As I LOOKED about me at the stark and cloud-topped hills, the waste of pressure-rippled ice, and, beyond the valley, to the desolate and treeless roll of tundra, I had no doubt that this was excellent wolf country. Indeed, I suspected that many pairs of lupine eyes were already watching me with speculative interest. I burrowed into my mountain of gear, found the revolver, and then took stock of my situation.

It did not seem very prepossessing. True, I had apparently penetrated to the heart of the Keewatin Barren Lands. And I had established a kind of base, although its location—on the lake ice, far from land—left much to be desired. So far, I had adhered strictly to the letter of my instructions; but the next paragraph in my operation order was a stickler.

Para. 3
  Sec. (C)
    Subpara. (iv)

Immediately after establishing a permanent base you will proceed, by means of canoe and utilizing waterways, to make an extensive general survey of the surrounding country to a depth, and in a manner, which will be significant in statistical terms, in order to determine the range/population ratio of Canis lupus and in order to establish contact with the study species. . . .

I was willing enough to carry on as per instructions, but the ice underfoot had a solidity about it which suggested that canoeing would have to be deferred for several weeks, if not forever. Furthermore, without some alternative means of transport, I did not seen how I could even begin the task of moving my mountain of gear to a permanent location on dry land. As to establishing contact with the study species—this seemed out of the question at the moment, unless the wolves themselves decided to take the initiative.

It was a serious dilemma. My orders had been drawn up for me after detailed consultation with the Meteorological Service, which had assured my Department that "normally" the lakes and rivers in the central Barrens could be expected to be clear of ice by the date of my arrival.

My orientation course in Ottawa had taught me that one never questioned information emanating from another department; and if a field operation based on such information went awry, it was invariably the fault of the fellow in the field.

Under the circumstances there was only one thing I could do. Despite the discouraging reaction I had had to my first radiogram to Ottawa, I had no alternative but to seek new orders once again.

Briskly I went to work uncovering the portable radio and setting it up on top of a pile of boxes. I had not previously had time to examine this instrument, and on opening the *Instruction Manual* I was a little taken aback to find that the model with which I had been supplied was intended for the use of forest rangers and could not normally be expected to work over ranges of more than twenty miles. Nevertheless I connected the batteries, rigged the aerial, turned knobs and pressed buttons according to instructions—and went on the air.

For some reason known only to the Department of

Transport, which licenses such mobile transmitters as mine, my call sign was "Daisy Mae." For the next hour Daisy Mae cried plaintively into the darkling subarctic skies, but without raising a whisper of a reply. I was almost ready to accept the pessimistic statement in the manual and give up the attempt as hopeless when I caught the faint echo of a human voice above the whistle and rustle of static in the earphones. Hastily I tuned the set until I could make out a gabble of words which it took me some time to identify as Spanish.

Since I realize that what I must now recount may strain the credulity of some of my readers; and since I have no technical knowledge whatsoever about radio, I can do no more than put forward an explanation given to me later by an expert, together with the assurance that no mere biologist could possibly have invented the sequence of events which followed. The technical explanation embraces a mysterious phenomenon known as "wave skip," whereby, because of a combination of atmospheric conditions, it is sometimes possible (particularly in the north) for very low-powered transmitters to span considerable distances. My set outdid itself. The station I raised belonged to an amateur operator in Peru.

His English was easily as imperfect as my Spanish, so that it was some time before we began to get through to each other, and even then he seemed convinced I was calling from somewhere near Tierra del Fuego. I was beginning to feel exceedingly frustrated before the Peruvian finally agreed to take down the substance of my message to my Chief, and forward it by commercial means to Ottawa. Recalling recent admonitions I kept this message to the ten-word minimum, which was probably just as well, for those ten words, inadequately understood in Peru,

and no doubt thoroughly corrupted by double trans-
lation, were sufficient to cause something of a crisis—
as I was to learn many months later.

Perhaps because of its South American origin the
message was delivered, not to my own department,
but to the Department of External Affairs. External
could make nothing of it, except that it seemed to
have come from Tierra del Fuego and it appeared to
be in code. Hurried inquiries embracing the Ministry
of Defense failed to identify the code, or to reveal
the presence of any known Canadian agent in the
Cape Horn region.

It was only through fortuitous circumstances that
the mystery was ever resolved. Some weeks later
one of the secretaries at External who was in the
habit of lunching with a senior man in my department
told him the story, and, in the telling, casually
mentioned that the inscrutable message was signed
VARLEY MONFAT.

With commendable and rather surprising acumen,
the senior man had identified me as the probable
originator of the message; but this only led to the
posing of a new and even more disturbing mystery,
since no one could be found who would admit to
having authorized me to go to Tierra del Fuego in
the first place. The upshot was that a series of urgent
messages were dispatched to me through the Canadian Counsul in Chile, instructing me to report to
Ottawa at once.

None of these messages ever reached me, nor
could they have done so even if they had been sent
by a more direct route, for the battery in my radio
was good for only six hours' use, and the only station
I was ever again able to raise before the batteries
went dead was broadcasting a light music program
from Moscow.

But to return to my narrative:

By the time I had finished my business with Peru,
it had begun to grow quite dark and the surrounding

hills seemed to be closing in on me. I had as yet seen no sign of wolves; but they were understandably very much on my mind, and when I glimpsed a flicker of distant movement near the valley mouth, I became even more wolf-conscious.

By straining my hearing I detected a faint but electrifying sound—one that I instantly recognized, for, though I had never before heard it in the wild, I *had* heard it several times in cowboy films. It was unmistakably the howling of a wolf pack in full cry, and, equally unmistakably, the pack was crying full in my direction. At least one of my problems appeared to have been solved. I was about to establish contact with the study species.

The solution of this problem led directly to the discovery of several new ones, not the least of which was that there were only six rounds in my pistol and I couldn't, for the life of me, remember where I had stowed the reserve ammunition. This was a matter of some moment, since I knew from my extensive reading on the subject that the number of individuals in a wolf pack can vary from four to forty. Furthermore, judging from the volume of sounds being made by the approaching animals, I suspected that *this* pack numbered closer to four hundred.

The subarctic night was now hard upon me, and the wolves soon would be too. It was already so dark that I could not see them clearly enough to estimate their actual numbers or gauge their probable behavior pattern. I therefore decided I should retire underneath the upturned canoe, so that the presence of a human being would not be readily apparent, with its consequent tendency to induce atypical behavior in the beasts.

Now one of the cardinal tenets of biology is that the observer must never allow his attention to be distracted; but honesty compels me to admit that under the present circumstances I found it difficult to maintain an attitude of correct scientific concentration. I was particularly worried about my canoe. Being lightly built of canvas over thin cedar staves, it might, I suspected, be easily damaged by rough usage, in which case I would be completely immobilized in the future. The second thing which was bothering me was so unusual that I must give it special emphasis, if only because it demonstrates the basic illogicality of the human mind when not under proper disciplinary control. I found myself fervently wishing I was a pregnant Eskimo.

Since I could no longer see what was happening, I had to rely upon my other senses. My ears kept me informed as the pack swept up at full speed, circled my pile of equipment once, and then rushed straight for the canoe.

A terrific chorus of howls, barks and yelps very nearly deafened me, and so confusing was the noise that I began to experience hallucinations, imagining I could hear the deep-throated roar of an almost human voice above the general tumult. The roar sounded rather like:

FURCRISAKESTOPYOUGODAMNSONSABITCHES!

At this point there was much scuffling, an outburst of pained yelping, and then, miraculously, total silence.

I had been trained for years to make accurate deductions from natural phenomena, but this situation was beyond me. I needed more data. Very cautiously I put one eye to the narrow slit between the gunwale of the canoe and the ice below. At first I could see nothing but wolf feet—scores of them; but then my glance fastened on another pair of feet— a *single* pair—which could have belonged to no wolf. My deductive abilities returned all of a rush. I lifted the side of the canoe, stuck out my head, and peered upward into the bewildered and rather apprehensive face of a young man clad all in caribou furs.

Scattered around him, and staring at me with deep suspicion, were the fourteen large and formidable Huskies which made up his team. But of bona fide wolves . . . there was not one in sight.

5

Contact!

NATURALLY I was disappointed that my first encounter with wolves should have turned out to be an encounter with nonwolves; but there were compensations.

The young man who owned the dogs was, so it developed, a trapper of mixed Eskimo and white parentage who possessed a cabin a few miles away. It was ideally suited to serve me as a permanent base camp. Apart from a small band of Eskimos including his mother's family, living seventy miles away to the north, this young man, whose name was Mike, was the only human inhabitant in an area of some ten thousand square miles. This was excellent news, for it ensured that my study of the wolves would not be adversely affected by human intrusions.

Mike was at first inclined to treat me with some reserve—not to say suspicion. During his eighteen years of life he had never known an aircraft to land in his part of the Barren Lands, and indeed had only seen two or three planes before, and these had been passing high overhead. It was therefore difficult for him to absorb the fact that an aircraft which he had neither seen nor heard had landed me and my immense pile of equipment on the middle of his lake. In the beginning of our relationship he leaned more toward a supernatural explanation of my presence; for he had learned enough about Christianity from his white trader father to be on his guard against the devil. Consequently he took no chances. During the first few days he carried his 30-30 rifle in his hands and kept his distance; but soon after I introduced him to wolf-juice he put the rifle away, having apparently decided that if I *was* the devil, my blandishments were too powerful to be resisted.

Probably because he could not think what else to do with me, Mike led me off to his cabin that first night. Although it was hardly a palatial affair, being built of poles and roofed with decaying caribou hides, I saw at once that it would serve my purposes.

Having been empowered by the Department to hire native assistance, so long as the consequent expenditure did not exceed three dollars a month, I promptly made a deal with Mike, giving him an official I.O.U. for ten dollars to cover three months' accommodation in his cabin, as well as his services as guide and general factotum. I was aware that it was a generous payment in the light of the prevailing rates which Government agencies, missions and the trading companies paid the arctic natives, but I felt my extravagance would be tolerated by the Treasury Department in view of the fact that, without Mike's help, my own Department stood to lose about four thousand dollars' worth of equipment as soon as the lake ice melted.

I suspect, from the nature of subsequent events, that the bargain I struck with Mike was rather one-sided and that he may not have fully grasped its implications; but in any event he provided the services of his dog team to help me move my supplies and equipment to his cabin.

During the next several days I was extremely busy unpacking my equipment and setting up my field laboratory—being obliged to usurp most of the limited space in the tiny cabin in the process. I had little time to spare for Mike, but I did notice that he seemed deeply preoccupied. However, since he had so far seemed to be naturally taciturn—except with his dogs—and because I did not feel it right, on such short acquaintance, to intrude into his personal affairs, I made no attempt to discover the nature of his distress. Nevertheless I did occasionally try to divert him by offering demonstrations of some of my scientific equipment.

These demonstrations seemed to fascinate him, although they did not have the desired effect of easing his distrait attitude which, if anything, got worse. Shortly after I showed him the cyanide "wolf getters" and explained that not only were they instantly fatal, but almost impossible to detect, he began to display definite signs of irrational behavior. He took to carrying a long stick about with him, and before he would even sit down at the crude table for a meal, he would poke the chair, and sometimes even the plate of food, in a most peculiar way. He would also poke at his boots and clothing before picking them up in the morning when he was getting dressed.

On another occasion, when I showed him four gross of mousetraps with which I intended to collect small mammals to be used in determining the identification of animal remains found in wolf stomachs, and then explained the method of boiling a mouse skeleton in order to prepare it as a museum specimen, he departed the cabin without a word and refused to take his meals with me from that time forward.

I was not unduly alarmed by his behavior, for I had some knowledge of psychology and I recognized the symptions of an ingrown personality. Nevertheless I determined to try to draw Mike out of himself. One evening I inveigled him over to the corner where I had set up my portable laboratory and proudly showed him my collection of glittering scalpels, bone shears, brain spoons and other intricate instruments which I would use in conducting autopsies on wolves, caribou and other beasts. I experienced some difficulty in explaining to Mike what was meant by an autopsy, so I opened a pathology textbook at a two-page color diagram of a human abdomen under dissection, and with this visual aid was well into my explanation when I realized I had lost my audience. Mike was backing slowly toward the door, his black eyes fixed on me with an expression of growing horror, and I realized at once that he had misconstrued what I had been saying. I sprang up in an attempt to reassure him, but at my movement he turned and fled through the door at a dead run.

I did not see him again until the following afternoon, when, returning from setting out a trapline for mice, I found him in the cabin packing his equipment as if for an extended journey. In a voice so low and rapid that I had difficulty understanding him, he explained that he had been urgently called away to visit his sick mother at the camp of the Eskimos, and would probably be gone for some time. With that he rushed out to where his team stood ready harnessed and, without another word, departed at a furious pace into the north.

I was sorry to see him go, for the knowledge that I was now entirely alone with the local wolves, while satisfying from a scientific point of view, seemed to intensify the *Hound of the Baskervilles* atmosphere of the desolate and stormswept lands around me. Then too, I had not yet clearly decided upon the best method of approaching the wolves, and I would have been happy to have had Mike perform the initial introductions. However, a sick mother took precedence even over my scientific needs—though I am still at a loss to understand how Mike knew his mother was ill.

The weighty problem of how best to make contact with the wolves hung fire while I began drawing up my study schedules. These were detailed in the extreme. Under "Sexual Behavior" alone I was able to list fifty-one subtopics, all requiring investigation. By the end of the week I was running short of paper. It was time to get out and about.

As I was a newcomer to the Barrens, it behooved me to familiarize myself with the country in a cautious manner. Hence, on my first expedition afield I contented myself with making a circular tour on a radius of about three hundred yards from the cabin.

This expedition revealed little except the presence of four or five hundred caribou skeletons; indeed, the entire area surrounding the cabin seemed to be carpeted in caribou bones. Since I knew from my researches in Churchill that trappers never shot caribou, I could only assume that these animals had been killed by wolves. This was a sobering conclusion. Assuming that the density of the caribou kill was uniform over the whole country, the sample I had seen indicated that wolves must kill, on the average, about twenty million caribou a year in Keewatin alone.

After this dismaying tour of the boneyard it was three days before I found time for another trip afield. Carrying a rifle and wearing my revolver, I went a quarter-mile on this second expedition—but saw no wolves. However, to my surprise I observed that the density of caribou remains decreased in an almost geometric ratio to the distance from the cabin. Sorely puzzled by the fact that the wolves seemed to have chosen to commit their worst slaughter so close to a human habitation, I resolved to question Mike about it if or when I saw him again.

Meantime spring had come to the Barrens with volcanic violence. The snows melted so fast that the frozen rivers could not carry the melted water, which flowed six feet deep on top of the ice. Finally the ice let go, with a thunderous explosion; then it promptly jammed, and in short order the river beside which I was living had entered into the cabin, bringing with it the accumulated refuse left by fourteen Huskies during a long winter.

Eventually the jam broke and the waters subsided; but the cabin had lost its charm, for the debris on the floor was a foot thick and somewhat repellent. I decided to pitch my tent on a gravel ridge above the cabin, and here I was vainly trying to go to sleep that evening when I became aware of unfamiliar sounds. Sitting bolt upright, I listened intently.

The sounds were coming from just across the river, to the north, and they were a weird medley of whines, whimpers and small howls. My grip on the rifle slowly relaxed. If there is one thing at which scientists are adept, it is learning from experience; I was not to be fooled twice. The cries were obviously those of a Husky, probably a young one, and I deduced that it must be one of Mike's dogs (he owned three half-grown pups not yet trained to harness which ran loose after the team) that had got lost, retraced its way to the cabin, and was now begging for someone to come and be nice to it.

I was delighted. If that pup needed a friend, a chum, I was its man! I climbed hastily into my clothes, ran down to the riverbank, launched the canoe, and paddled lustily for the far bank.

The pup had never ceased its mournful plaint, and I was about to call out reassuringly when it occurred to me that an unfamiliar human voice might frighten it. I decided to stalk it instead, and to betray my presence only when I was close enough for soothing murmurs.

From the nature of the sounds I had assumed the dog was only a few yards away from the far bank, but as I made my way in the dim half-light, over broken boulders and across gravel ridges, the sounds seemed to remain at the same volume while I appeared to be getting no closer. I assumed the pup was retreating, perhaps out of shyness. In my anxiety not to startle it away entirely, I still kept quiet, even when the whimpering wail stopped, leaving me uncertain about the right direction to pursue. However, I saw a steep ridge looming ahead of me and I suspected that, once I gained its summit, I would have a clear enough view to enable me to locate the lost animal. As I neared the crest of the ridge I got down on my stomach (practicing the fieldcraft I had learned in the Boy Scouts) and cautiously inched my way the last few feet.

My head came slowly over the crest—and there was my quarry. He was lying down, evidently resting after his mournful singsong, and his nose was about six feet from mine. We stared at one another in silence. I do not know what went on in his massive skull, but my head was full of the most disturbing thoughts. I was peering straight into the amber gaze of a fully grown arctic wolf, who probably weighed more than I did, and who was certainly a lot better versed in close-combat techniques than I would ever be.

For some seconds neither of us moved but continued to stare hypnotically into one another's eyes. The wolf was the first to break the spell. With a spring which would have done justice to a Russian dancer, he leaped about a yard straight into the air and came down running. The textbooks say a wolf can run twenty-five miles an hour, but this one did not appear to be running, so much as flying low. Within seconds he had vanished from my sight.

My own reaction was not so dramatic, although I may very well have set some sort of a record for a cross-country traverse myself. My return over the river was accomplished with such verve that I paddled the canoe almost her full length up on the beach on the other side. Then, remembering my responsibilities to my scientific supplies, I entered the cabin, barred the door, and regardless of the discomfort caused by the stench of the debris on the floor made myself as comfortable as I could on top of the table for the balance of the short-lived night.

It had been a strenuous interlude, but I could congratulate myself that I had, at last, established contact—no matter how briefly—with the study species.

6

The Den

WHAT WITH one thing and another I found it difficult to get to sleep. The table was too short and too hard; the atmosphere in the cabin was far too thick; and the memory of my recent encounter with the wolf was too vivid. I tried counting sheep, but they kept turning into wolves, leaving me more wakeful than ever. Finally, when some red-backed mice who lived under the floor began to produce noises which were realistic approximations of the sounds a wolf might make if he were snuffling at the door, I gave up all idea of sleep, lit Mike's oil lantern, and resigned myself to waiting for the dawn.

I allowed my thoughts to return to the events of the evening. Considering how brief the encounter with the wolf had been, I was amazed to discover the wealth of detail I could recall. In my mind's eye I could visualize the wolf as if I had known him (or her) for years. The image of that massive head with its broad white ruff, short pricked ears, tawny eyes and grizzled muzzle was indelibly fixed in memory. So too was the image of the wolf in flight; the lean and sinewy motion and the overall impression of a beast the size of a small pony; an impression implicit with a feeling of lethal strength.

The more I thought about it, the more I realized that I had not cut a very courageous figure. My withdrawal from the scene had been hasty and devoid of dignity. But then the compensating thought occurred to me that the wolf had not stood upon the

38

order of his (her) going either, and I began to feel
somewhat better; a state of mind which may have been
coincidental with the rising of the sun, which was now
illuminating the bleak world outside my window with
a gray and pallid light.

As the light grew stronger I even began to suspect
that I had muffed an opportunity—one which might,
moreover, never again recur. It was borne in upon
me that I should have followed the wolf and
endeavored to gain his confidence, or at least to convince him that I harbored no ill will toward his kind.

The Canada jays who came each day to scavenge
the debris in the dooryard were now becoming active. I lit the stove and cooked my breakfast. Then,
filled with resolution, I packed some grub in a haver-
sack, saw to the supply of ammunition for my rifle
and revolver, slung my binoculars around my neck,
and set out to make good my failure of the previous
evening. My plan was straightforward. I intended to
go directly to the spot where I had seen the wolf
disappear, pick up his trail, and follow until I found
him.

The going was rough and rocky at first, and I took
a good deal longer to cover the intervening ground
than the wolf had done, but eventually I scaled the
low crest where I had last seen him (or her). Ahead
of me I found a vast expanse of boggy muskeg which
promised well for tracks; and indeed I found a set
of footprints almost immediately, leading off across
a patch of chocolate-colored bog.

I should have felt overjoyed, yet somehow I did
not. The truth is that my first sight of the wolf's
paw-prints was a revelation for which I was quite
unprepared. It is one thing to read in a textbook
that the footprints of an arctic wolf measure six inches
in diameter; but it is quite another thing to see them
laid out before you in all their bald immensity. It
has a dampening effect on one's enthusiasm. The
mammoth prints before me, combined as they were

with a forty-inch stride, suggested that the beast I was proposing to pursue was built on approximately the scale of a grizzly bear.

I studied those prints for quite a long time, and might perhaps have studied them for even longer had I not made the discovery that I had neglected to bring my pocket compass with me. Since it would have been foolhardy to proceed into an unmarked wilderness without it, I regretfully decided to return to the cabin.

When I got back to Mike's the compass was not where I had left it. In fact I couldn't remember where I *had* left it, or even if I had seen it since leaving Ottawa. It was an impasse; but in order not to waste my time I got down one of the standard works with which the Department had equipped me, and consulted the section on wolves. I had, of course, read this section many times before, but some of the salient facts had evidently failed to impress themselves clearly on my mind. Now, with my capacity for mental imagery sharpened by my first look at a set of real wolf tracks, I reread the piece with new interest and appreciation.

Arctic wolves, the author informed me, were the largest of the many subspecies or races of *Canis lupus*. Specimens had been examined which weighed one hundred and seventy pounds; which measured eight feet seven inches from tip of nose to tip of tail; and which stood forty-two inches high at the shoulders. An adult of the arctic race could eat (and presumably did on favorable occasions) thirty pounds of raw meat at a sitting. The teeth were "massive in construction and capable of both rending and grinding action, which enables the owner to dismember the largest mammals with ease, and crush even the strongest bones." The section closed with the following succinct remarks: "The wolf is a savage, powerful killer. It is one of the most feared and hated animals known to man, and with excellent reason."

The reason was not given, but it would have been superfluous in any case.

I was very thoughtful for the balance of the day, and there were moments when I wondered if my hopes of gaining the confidence of the wolves might not be overly optimistic. As to demonstrating that I bore them no ill will—this I felt would be easy enough to do, but would be of little value unless the wolves felt like reciprocating.

The next morning I undertook to clean up the Stygian mess in the cabin, and in the process I uncovered my compass. I set it on the windowsill while I continued with my work, but the sun caught its brass surface and it glittered at me so accusingly that I resigned myself to making another effort to restore the lost contact between me and the wolves.

My progress on this second safari was even slower, since I was carrying my rifle, shotgun, pistol and pistol belt, a small hatchet and my hunting knife, together with a flask of wolf-juice in case I fell into one of the icy streams.

It was a hot day, and spring days in the subarctic can be nearly as hot as in the tropics. The first mosquitoes were already heralding the approach of the sky-filling swarms which would soon make travel on the Barrens a veritable trip through hell. I located the wolf tracks and resolutely set out upon the trail.

It led directly across the muskeg for several miles; but although the wolf had sunk in only three or four inches, my steps sank in until I reached solid ice a foot beneath the surface. It was with great relief that I finally breasted another gravel ridge and lost all trace of the wolf tracks.

My attempts to find them again were perfunctory. As I gazed around me at the morose world of rolling muskeg and frost-shattered stone that stretched un-interruptedly to a horizon so distant it might as well have been the horizon of the sea, I felt lonelier than I had ever felt in all my life. No friendly sound of aircraft engines broke the silence of that empty sky. No distant rumble of traffic set the ground beneath my feet to shaking. Only the disembodied whistling of an unseen plover gave any indication that life existed anywhere in all this lunar land where no tree grew.

I found a niche amongst some lichen-covered rocks and, having firmly jammed myself into it, ate and drank my lunch. Then I picked up the binoculars and began to scan the barren landscape for some signs of life.

Directly in front of me was the ice-covered bay of a great lake, and on the far side of this bay was something which at least relieved the somber monochrome of the muskeg colorings. It was a yellow sand esker, rising to a height of fifty or sixty feet and winding sinuously away into the distance like a gigantic snake.

These barren land eskers are the inverted beds of long-vanished rivers which once flowed through and over the glaciers that, ten thousand years ago, covered the Keewatin Barrens to a depth of several thousand feet. When the ice melted, sandy riverbeds were deposited on the land below, where they now provide almost the sole visual relief in the bleak monotony of the tundra plains.

I gazed at this one with affection, studying it closely; and as I swept it with my glasses I saw something move. The distance was great, but the impression I had was of someone, just the other side of the esker crest, waving his arm above his head. Much excited, I stumbled to my feet and trotted along the ridge to its termination on the shore of the bay. I was then not more than three hundred yards from the esker and when I got my breath back I took another look through the glasses.

The object I had previously glimpsed was still in

view, but now it looked like a white feather boa being vehemently waved by persons or person unseen. It was a most inexplicable object, and nothing I had ever heard of in my study of natural history seemed to fit it. As I stared in perplexity, the first boa was joined by a second one, also waving furiously, and both boas began to move slowly along, parallel to the crest of the esker.

I began to feel somewhat uneasy, for here was a phenomenon which did not seem to be subject to scientific explanation. In fact I was on the point of abandoning my interest in the spectacle until some expert in psychic research happened along—when, without warning, both boas turned toward me, began rising higher and higher, and finally revealed themselves as the tails of two wolves proceeding to top the esker.

The esker overlooked my position on the bay's shore, and I felt as nakedly exposed as the lady in the famous brassiére advertisement. Hunkering down to make myself as small as possible, I wormed my way into the rocks and did my best to be unobtrusive. I need not have worried. The wolves paid no attention to me, if indeed they even saw me. They were far too engrossed in their own affairs, which, as I slowly and incredulously began to realize, were at that moment centered around the playing of a game of tag.

It was difficult to believe my eyes. They were romping like a pair of month-old pups! The smaller wolf (who soon gave concrete evidence that she was a female) took the initiative. Putting her head down on her forepaws and elevating her posterior in a most undignified manner, she suddenly pounced toward the much larger male whom I now recognized as my acquaintance of two days earlier. He, in his attempt to evade her, tripped and went sprawling. Instantly she was upon him, nipping him smartly in the backside, before leaping away to run around him in frenzied circles. The male scrambled to his feet and gave chase, but only by the most strenuous efforts was he able to close the gap until he, in his turn, was able to nip *her* backside. Thereupon the roles were again reversed, and the female began to pursue the male, who led her on a wild scrabble up, over, down, and back across the esker until finally both wolves lost their footing on the steep slope and went skidding down it inextricably locked together.

When they reached the bottom they separated, shook the sand out of their hair, and stood panting heavily, almost nose to nose. Then the female reared up and quite literally embraced the male with both forepaws while she proceeded to smother him in long-tongued kisses.

The male appeared to be enduring this overt display of affection, rather than enjoying it. He kept trying to avert his head, to no avail. Involuntarily I felt my sympathy warming toward him, for, in truth, it was a disgusting exhibition of wanton passion. Nevertheless he bore it with what stoicism he could muster until the female tired. Turning from him, she climbed halfway up the esker slope and ... disappeared.

She seemed to have vanished off the face of the earth without leaving a trace behind her. Not until I swung the glasses back toward a dark shadow in a fold of the esker near where I had last seen her did I understand. The dark shadow was the mouth of a cave, or den, and the female wolf had almost certainly gone into it.

I was so elated by the realization that I had not only located a pair of wolves, but by an incredible stroke of fortune had found their den as well, that I forgot all caution and ran to a nearby knoll in order to gain a better view of the den mouth.

The male wolf, who had been loafing about the foot of the esker after the departure of his wife, instantly saw me. In three or four bounds he reached the ridge of the esker, where he stood facing me in an attitude of tense and threatening vigilance. As I looked up at him my sense of exhilaration waned rapidly. He no longer seemed like a playful pup, but had metamorphosed into a magnificent engine of destruction which impressed me so much that the neck of my flask positively rattled against my teeth.

I decided I had better not disturb the wolf family any more that day, for fear of upsetting them and perhaps forcing them to move away. So I withdrew. It was not an easy withdrawal, for one of the most difficult things I know of is to walk backward up a broken rocky slope for three quarters of a mile encumbered, as I was, by the complex hardware of a scientist's trade.

When I reached the ridge from which I had first seen the wolves I took a last quick look through the binoculars. The female was still invisible, and the male had so far relaxed his attitude of vigilance as to lie down on the crest of the esker. While I watched he turned around two or three times, as a dog will, and then settled himself, nose under tail, with the evident intention of having a nap.

I was much relieved to see he was no longer interested in me, for it would have been a tragedy if my accidental intrusion had unduly disturbed these wolves, thereby prejudicing what promised to be a unique opportunity to study the beasts I had come so far to find.

7

The Watcher Watched

THE LACK OF sustained interest which the big male wolf had displayed toward me was encouraging enough to tempt me to visit the den again the next morning; but this time, instead of the shotgun and the hatchet (I still retained the rifle, pistol and hunting knife) I carried a high-powered periscopic telescope and a tripod on which to mount it.

It was a fine sunny morning with enough breeze to keep the mosquito vanguard down. When I reached the bay where the esker was, I chose a prominent knoll of rock some four hundred yards from the den, behind which I could set up my telescope so that its objective lenses peered over the crest, but left me in hiding. Using consummate fieldcraft, I approached the chosen observation point in such a manner that the wolves could not possibly have seen me and, since the wind was from them to me, I was assured that they would have had no suspicion of my arrival.

When all was in order, I focused the telescope; but to my chagrin I could see no wolves. The magnification of the instrument was such that I could almost distinguish the individual grains of sand in the esker; yet, though I searched every inch of it for a distance of a mile on each side of the den, I could find no indication that wolves were about, or had ever been about. By noon, I had a bad case of eyestrain and a worse one of cramps, and I had almost concluded that my hypothesis of the previous day was grievously at fault and that the "den" was just a fortuitous hole in the sand.

This was discouraging, for it had begun to dawn on me that all of the intricate study plans and schedules which I had drawn up were not going to be of much use without a great deal of co-operation on the part of the wolves. In country as open and as vast as this one was, the prospects of getting within visual range of a wolf except by the luckiest of accidents (and I had already had more than my ration of these) were negligible. I realized that if this was not a wolves' den which I had found, I had about as much chance of locating the actual den in this faceless wilderness as I had of finding a diamond mine.

Glumly I went back to my unproductive survey through the telescope. The esker remained deserted. The hot sand began sending up heat waves which increased my eyestrain. By 2:00 P.M. I had given up hope. There seemed no further point in concealment, so I got stiffly to my feet and prepared to relieve myself.

Now it is a remarkable fact that a man, even though he may be alone in a small boat in mid-ocean, or isolated in the midst of the trackless forest, finds that the very process of unbuttoning causes him to become peculiarly sensitive to the possibility that he may be under observation. At this critical juncture none but the most self-assured of men, no matter how certain he may be of his privacy, can refrain from casting a surreptitious glance around to reassure himself that he really is alone.

To say I was chagrined to discover I was *not* alone would be an understatement; for sitting directly behind me, and not twenty yards away, were the missing wolves.

They appeared to be quite relaxed and comfortable, as if they had been sitting there behind my back for hours. The big male seemed a trifle bored; but the female's gaze was fixed on me with what I took to be an expression of unabashed and even prurient curiosity.

The human psyche is truly an amazing thing. Under almost any other circumstances I would probably have been panic-stricken, and I think few would have blamed me for it. But these were not ordinary circumstances and my reaction was one of violent indignation. Outraged, I turned my back on the watching wolves and with fingers which were shaking with vexation, hurriedly did up my buttons. When decency, if not my dignity, had been restored, I rounded on those wolves with a virulence which surprised even me.

"Shoo!" I screamed at them. "What the hell do you think you're at, you . . . you . . . peeping Toms! Go away, for heaven's sake!"

The wolves were startled. They sprang to their feet, glanced at each other with a wild surmise, and then trotted off, passed down a draw, and disappeared in the direction of the esker. They did not once look back.

With their departure I experienced a reaction of another kind. The realization that they had been sitting almost within jumping distance of my unprotected back for God knows how long set up such a turmoil of the spirit that I had to give up all thought of carrying on where my discovery of the wolves had forced me to leave off. Suffering from both mental and physical strain, therefore, I hurriedly packed my gear and set out for the cabin.

My thoughts that evening were confused. True, my prayer had been answered, and the wolves had certainly co-operated by reappearing; but on the other hand I was becoming prey to a small but nagging doubt as to just *who* was watching *whom*. I felt that I, because of my specific superiority as a member of *Homo sapiens*, together with my intensive technical training, was entitled to pride of place. The sneaking suspicion that this pride had been denied and that, in point of fact, *I* was the one who was under observation, had an unsettling effect upon my ego.

In order to establish my ascendancy once and for all, I determined to visit the wolf esker itself the following morning and make a detailed examination of the presumed den. I decided to go by canoe, since the rivers were now clear and the rafting lake ice was being driven offshore by a stiff northerly breeze.

It was a fine, leisurely trip to Wolf House Bay, as I had now named it. The annual spring caribou migration north from the forested areas of Manitoba toward the distant tundra plains near Dubawnt Lake was under way, and from my canoe I could see countless skeins of caribou crisscrossing the muskegs and the rolling hills in all directions. No wolves were in evidence as I neared the esker, and I assumed they were away hunting a caribou for lunch.

I ran the canoe ashore and, fearfully laden with cameras, guns, binoculars and other gear, laboriously climbed the shifting sands of the esker to the shadowy place where the female wolf had disappeared. En route I found unmistakable proof that this esker was, if not the home, at least one of the favorite promenades of the wolves. It was liberally strewn with scats and covered with wolf tracks which in many places formed well-defined paths.

The den was located in a small wadi in the esker, and was so well concealed that I was on the point of walking past without seeing it, when a series of small squeaks attracted my attention. I stopped and turned to look, and there, not fifteen feet below me, were four small, gray beasties engaged in a free-for-all wrestling match.

At first I did not recognize them for what they

were. The fat, fox faces with pinprick ears; the butterball bodies, as round as pumpkins; the short, bowed legs and the tiny upthrust sprigs of tails were so far from my conception of a wolf that my brain refused to make the logical connection.

Suddenly one of the pups caught my scent. He stopped in the midst of attempting to bite off a brother's tail and turned smoky blue eyes up toward me. What he saw evidently intrigued him. Lurching free of the scrimmage, he padded toward me with a rolling, wobbly gait; but a flea bit him unexpectedly before he had gone far, and he had to sit down to scratch it.

At this instant an adult wolf let loose a full-throated howl vibrant with alarm and warning, not more than fifty yards from me.

The idyllic scene exploded into frenzied action.

The pups became gray streaks which vanished into the gaping darkness of the den mouth. I spun around to face the adult wolf, lost my footing, and started to skid down the loose slope toward the den. In trying to regain my balance I thrust the muzzle of the rifle deep into the sand, where it stuck fast until the carrying-strap dragged it free as I slid rapidly away from it. I fumbled wildly at my revolver, but so cluttered was I with cameras and equipment straps that I did not succeed in getting the weapon clear as, accompanied by a growing avalanche of sand, I shot past the den mouth, over the lip of the main ridge and down the full length of the esker slope. Miraculously, I kept my feet; but only by dint of superhuman contortions during which I was alternately bent forward like a skier going over a jump, or leaning backward at such an acute angle I thought my backbone was going to snap.

It must have been quite a show. When I got myself straightened out and glanced back up the esker, it was to see *three* adult wolves ranged side by side like spectators in the Royal Box, all peering down at me with expressions of incredulous delight.

I lost my temper. This is something a scientist seldom does, but I lost mine. My dignity had been too heavily eroded during the past several days and my scientific detachment was no longer equal to the strain. With a snarl of exasperation I raised the rifle but, fortunately, the thing was so clogged with sand that when I pressed the trigger nothing happened.

The wolves did not appear alarmed until they saw me begin to dance up and down in helpless fury, waving the useless rifle and hurling imprecations at their cocked ears; whereupon they exchanged quizzical looks and silently withdrew out of my sight.

I too withdrew, for I was in no fit mental state to carry on with my exacting scientific duties. To tell the truth, I was in no fit mental state to do anything except hurry home to Mike's and seek solace for my tattered nerves and frayed vanity in the bottom of a jar of wolf-juice.

I had a long and salutary session with the stuff that night, and as my spiritual bruises became less painful under its healing influence I reviewed the incidents of the past few days. Inescapably, the realization was being borne in upon my preconditioned mind that the centuries-old and universally accepted human concept of wolf character was a palpable lie. On three separate occasions in less than a week I had been completely at the mercy of these "savage killers"; but far from attempting to tear me limb from limb, they had displayed a restraint verging on contempt, even when I invaded their home and appeared to be posing a direct threat to the young pups.

This much was obvious, yet I was still strangely reluctant to let the myth go down the drain. Part of this reluctance was no doubt due to the thought that, by discarding the accepted concepts of wolf nature, I would be committing scientific treason; part of it to the knowledge that recognition of the truth would deprive my mission of its fine aura of danger and high adventure; and not the least part of that reluctance was probably due to my unwillingness to accept the fact that I had been made to look like a blithering idiot—not by my fellow man, but by mere brute beasts.

Nevertheless I persevered.

When I emerged from my session with the wolf-juice the following morning I was somewhat the worse for wear in a physical sense; but I was cleansed and purified spiritually. I had wrestled with my devils and I had won. I had made my decision that, from this hour onward, I would go open-minded into the lupine world and learn to see and know the wolves, not for what they were supposed to be, but for what they actually were.

8

Staking the Land

DURING THE next several weeks I put my decision
into effect with the thoroughness for which I have
always been noted. I went completely to the wolves.
To begin with I set up a den of my own as near to
the wolves as I could conveniently get without disturbing the even tenor of their lives too much. After
all, I *was* a stranger, and an unwolflike one, so I did
not feel I should go too far too fast.

Abandoning Mike's cabin (with considerable relief, since as the days warmed up so did the smell)
I took a tiny tent and set it up on the shore of the
bay immediately opposite to the den esker. I kept
my camping gear to the barest minimum—a small
primus stove, a stew pot, a teakettle, and a sleeping
bag were the essentials. I took no weapons of any
kind, although there were times when I regretted
this omission, even if only fleetingly. The big telescope was set up in the mouth of the tent in such a
way that I could observe the den by day or night
without even getting out of my sleeping bag.

During the first days of my sojourn with the
wolves I stayed inside the tent except for brief and
necessary vists to the out-of-doors which I always
undertook when the wolves were not in sight. The
point of this personal concealment was to allow the
animals to get used to the tent and to accept it as
only another bump on a very bumpy piece of terrain.
Later, when the mosquito population reached full
flowering, I stayed in the tent practically all of the

time unless there was a strong wind blowing, for the most bloodthirsty beasts in the Arctic are not wolves, but the insatiable mosquitoes.

My precautions against disturbing the wolves were superfluous. It had required a week for me to get their measure, but they must have taken mine at our first meeting; and, while there was nothing overtly disdainful in their evident assessment of me, they managed to ignore my presence, and indeed my very existence, with a thoroughness which was somehow disconcerting.

Quite by accident I had pitched my tent within ten yards of one of the major paths used by the wolves when they were going to, or coming from, their hunting grounds to the westward; and only a few hours after I had taken up residence one of the wolves came back from a trip and discovered me and my tent. He was at the end of a hard night's work and was clearly tired and anxious to go home to bed. He came over a small rise fifty yards from me with his head down, his eyes half-closed, and a preoccupied air about him. Far from being the pre-ternaturally alert and suspicious beast of fiction, this wolf was so self-engrossed that he came straight on to within fifteen yards of me, and might have gone right past the tent without seeing it at all, had I not banged my elbow against the teakettle, making a resounding clank. The wolf's head came up and his eyes opened wide, but he did not stop or falter in his pace. One brief, sidelong glance was all he vouchsafed to me as he continued on his way.

It was true that I wanted to be inconspicuous, but I felt uncomfortable at being so totally ignored. Nevertheless, during the two weeks which followed, one or more wolves used the track past my tent almost every night—and never, except on one memorable occasion, did they evince the slightest interest in me.

By the time this happened I had learned a good deal about my wolfish neighbors, and one of the facts which had emerged was that they were not nomadic roamers, as is almost universally believed, but were settled beasts and the possessors of a large permanent estate with very definite boundaries.

The territory owned by my wolf family comprised more than a hundred square miles, bounded on one side by a river but otherwise not delimited by geographical features. Nevertheless there *were* boundaries, clearly indicated in wolfish fashion.

Anyone who has observed a dog doing his neighborhood rounds and leaving his personal mark on each convenient post will have already guessed how the wolves marked out *their* property. Once a week, more or less, the clan made the rounds of the family lands and freshened up the boundary markers—a sort of lupine beating of the bounds. This careful attention to property rights was perhaps made necessary by the presence of two other wolf families whose lands abutted on ours, although I never discovered any evidence of bickering or disagreements between the owners of the various adjoining estates. I suspect, therefore, that it was more of a ritual activity.

In any event, once I had become aware of the strong feeling of property rights which existed amongst the wolves, I decided to use this knowledge to make them at least recognize my existence. One evening, after they had gone off for their regular nightly hunt, I staked out a property claim of my own, embracing perhaps three acres, with the tent at the middle, and *including a hundred-yard long section of the wolves' path.*

Staking the land turned out to be rather more difficult than I had anticipated. In order to ensure that my claim would not be overlooked, I felt obliged to make a property mark on stones, clumps of moss, and patches of vegetation at intervals of not more than fifteen feet around the circumference of my claim. This took most of the night and required frequent returns to the tent to consume copious quantities of tea; but before dawn brought the hunters home the task was done, and I retired, somewhat exhausted, to observe results.

I had not long to wait. At 0814 hours, according to my wolf log, the leading male of the clan appeared over the ridge behind me, padding homeward with his usual air of preoccupation. As usual he did not deign to glance at the tent; but when he reached the point where my property line intersected the trail, he stopped as abruptly as if he had run into an invisible wall. He was only fifty yards from me and with my binoculars I could see his expression very clearly.

His attitude of fatigue vanished and was replaced by a look of bewilderment. Cautiously he extended his nose and sniffed at one of my marked bushes. He did not seem to know what to make of it or what to do about it. After a minute of complete indecision he backed away a few yards and sat down. And then, finally, he looked directly at the tent and at me. It was a long, thoughtful, considering sort of look.

Having achieved my object—that of forcing at least one of the wolves to take cognizance of my existence—I now began to wonder if, in my ignorance, I had transgressed some unknown wolf law of major importance and would have to pay for my temerity. I found myself regretting the absence of a weapon as the look I was getting became longer, yet more thoughtful, and still more intent.

I began to grow decidedly fidgety, for I dislike staring matches, and in this particular case I was up against a master, whose yellow glare seemed to become more baleful as I attempted to stare him down.

The situation was becoming intolerable. In an effort to break the impasse I loudly cleared my throat and turned my back on the wolf (for a tenth of a second) to indicate as clearly as possible that I found his continued scrutiny impolite, if not actually offensive.

He appeared to take the hint. Getting to his feet he had another sniff at my marker, and then he seemed to make up his mind. Briskly, and with an air of decision, he turned his attention away from me and began a systematic tour of the area I had staked out as my own. As he came to each boundary marker he sniffed it once or twice, then carefully placed *his* mark on the outside of each clump of grass or stone. As I watched I saw where I, in my ignorance, had erred. He made his mark with such economy that he was able to complete the entire circuit without having to reload once, or, to change the simile slightly, he did it all on one tank of fuel.

The task completed—and it had taken him no longer than fifteen minutes—he rejoined the path at the point where it left my property and trotted off towards his home—leaving me with a good deal to occupy my thoughts.

9

Good Old Uncle Albert

ONCE IT HAD been formally established and its existence ratified by the wolves themselves, my little enclave in their territory remained inviolate. Never again did a wolf trespass on my domain. Occasionally, one in passing would stop to freshen up some of the boundary marks on his side of the line, and, not to be outdone in ceremony, I followed suit to the best of my ability. Any lingering doubts I might have had as to my personal safety dissolved, and I was free to devote all my attention to the study of the beasts themselves.

Very early in my observations I discovered that they led a well-regulated life, although they were not slavish adherents to fixed schedules. Early in the evenings the males went off to work. They might depart at four o'clock or they might delay until six or seven, but sooner or later off they went on the nightly hunt. During this hunt they ranged far afield, although always—as far as I could tell—staying within the limits of the family territory. I estimated that during a normal hunt they covered thirty or forty miles before dawn. When times were hard they probably covered even greater distances, since on some occasions they did not get home until the afternoon. During the balance of the daylight hours they slept—but in their own peculiarly wolfish way, which consisted of curling up for short wolf-naps of from five to ten minutes' duration; after each of which they would take a quick look about, and then turn round once or twice before dozing off again.

The females and the pups led a more diurnal life. Once the males had departed in the evening, the female usually went into the den and stayed there, emerging only occasionally for a breath of air, a drink, or sometimes for a visit to the meat cache for a snack.

This cache deserves special mention. No food was ever stored or left close to the den; and only enough was brought in at one time for immediate consumption. Any surplus from a hunt was carried to the cache, which was located in a jumble of boulders half-a-mile from the den, and stuffed into crevices, primarily for the use of the nursing female who, of course, could not join the male wolves on extended hunting trips.

The cache was also used surreptitiously by a pair of foxes who had their own den close by. The wolves must have known of the location of the foxes' home, and probably knew perfectly well that there was a certain amount of pilfering from their cache; but they did nothing about it even though it would have been a simple matter for them to dig out and destroy the litter of fox pups. The foxes, on their side, seemed to have no fear of the wolves, and several times I saw one flit like a shadow across the esker within a few yards of a wolf without eliciting any response.

Later I concluded that almost all the dens used by the Barren Land wolves were abandoned fox burrows which had been taken over and enlarged by the wolves. It is possible that the usefulness of the foxes as preliminary excavators may have guaranteed them immunity; but it seems more likely that the wolves' tolerance simply reflected their general amiability.

During the day, while the male wolves took it easy, the female would be reasonably active about her household chores. Emerging boisterously from the close confines of the den, the pups also became active—to the point of total exhaustion. Thus throughout the entire twenty-four-hour period there was usually something going on, or at least the expectation of something, to keep me glued to the telescope.

After the first two days and nights of nearly continuous observing I had about reached the limits of my endurance. It was a most frustrating situation. I did not dare to go to sleep for fear of missing something vital. On the other hand, I became so sleepy that I was seeing double, if not triple, on occasion; although this effect may have been associated with the quantities of wolf-juice which I consumed in an effort to stay awake.

I saw that something drastic would have to be done or my whole study program would founder. I could think of nothing adequate until, watching one of the males dozing comfortably on a hillock near the den, I recognized the solution to my problem. It was simple. I had only to learn to nap like a wolf.

It took some time to get the knack of it. I experimented by closing my eyes and trying to wake up again five minutes later, but it didn't work. After the first two or three naps I failed to wake up at all until several hours had passed.

The fault was mine, for I had failed to imitate *all* the actions of a dozing wolf, and, as I eventually discovered, the business of curling up to start with, and spinning about after each nap, was vital to success. I don't know why this is so. Perhaps changing the position of the body helps to keep the circulation stimulated. I *do* know, however, that a series of properly conducted wolf-naps is infinitely more refreshing than the unconscious coma of seven or eight hours' duration which represents the human answer to the need for rest.

Unfortunately, the wolf-nap does not readily lend itself to adaptation into our society, as I discovered after my return to civilization when a young lady of whom I was enamored at the time parted company with me. She had rather, she told me vehemently, spend her life with a grasshopper who had rickets, than spend one more night in bed with me.

As I grew more completely attuned to their daily round of family life I found it increasingly difficult to maintain an impersonal attitude toward the wolves. No matter how hard I tried to regard them with scientific objectivity, I could not resist the impact of their individual personalities. Because he reminded me irresistibly of a Royal Gentleman for whom I worked as a simple soldier during the war, I found myself calling the father of the family George, even though in my notebooks, he was austerely identified only as Wolf "A."

George was a massive and eminently regal beast whose coat was silver-white. He was about a third larger than his mate, but he hardly needed this extra bulk to emphasize his air of masterful certainty. George had presence. His dignity was unassailable, yet he was by no means aloof. Conscientious to a fault, thoughtful of others, and affectionate within reasonable bounds, he was the kind of father whose idealized image appears in many wistful books of human family reminiscences, but whose real prototype has seldom paced the earth upon two legs. George was, in brief, the kind of father every son longs to acknowledge as his own.

His wife was equally memorable. A slim, almost pure-white wolf with a thick ruff around her face, and wide-spaced, slightly slanted eyes, she seemed the picture of a minx. Beautiful, ebullient, passionate to a degree, and devilish when the mood was on her, she hardly looked like the epitome of motherhood; yet there could have been no better mother anywhere. I found myself calling her Angeline, although I have never been able to trace the origin of that name in the murky depths of my own subconscious. I respected and liked George very much, but I became deeply fond of Angeline, and still live in hopes that I can somewhere find a human female who embodies all her virtues.

Angeline and George seemed as devoted a mated pair as one could hope to find. As far as I could tell they never quarreled, and the delight with which they greeted each other after even a short absence was obviously unfeigned. They were extremely affectionate with one another, but, alas, the many pages in my notebook which had been hopefully reserved for detailed comments on the sexual behavior and activities of wolves remained obstinately blank as far as George and Angeline were concerned.

Distressing as it was to my expectations, I discovered that physical lovemaking enters into the lives of a pair of mated wolves only during a period of two or three weeks early in the spring, usually in March. Virgin females (and they are all virginal until their second year) then mate; but unlike dogs, who have adopted many of the habits of their human owners, wolf bitches mate with only a single male, and mate for life.

Whereas the phrase "till death us do part" is one of the more amusing mockeries in the nuptial arrangements of a large proportion of the human race, with wolves it is a simple fact. Wolves are also strict monogamists, and although I do not necessarily consider this an admirable trait, it does make the reputation for unbridled promiscuity which we have bestowed on the wolf somewhat hypocritical.

While it was not possible for me to know with exact certainty how long George and Angeline had been mated, I was later able to discover from Mike that they had been together for at least five years— or the equivalent of thirty years in terms of the relative longevity of wolves and men. Mike and the Eskimos recognized the wolves in their area as familiar individuals, and the Eskimos (but not Mike) held the wolves in such high regard that they would not have thought of killing them or doing them an injury. Thus not only were George, Angeline and other members of the family well known to the Eskimos, but the site of their den had been known for some forty or fifty years, during which time generations of wolves had raised families there.

One factor concerning the organization of the family mystified me very much at first. During my early visit to the den I had seen *three* adult wolves; and during the first few days of observing the den I had again glimpsed the odd-wolf-out several times. He posed a major conundrum, for while I could accept the idea of a contented domestic group consisting of mated male and female and a bevy of pups, I had not yet progressed far enough into the wolf world to be able to explain, or to accept, the apparent existence of an eternal triangle.

Whoever the third wolf was, he was definitely a character. He was smaller than George, not so lithe and vigorous, and with a gray overcast to his otherwise white coat. He became "Uncle Albert" to me after the first time I saw him with the pups.

The sixth morning of my vigil had dawned bright and sunny, and Angeline and the pups took advantage of the good weather. Hardly was the sun risen (at three A.M.) when they all left the den and adjourned to a nearby sandy knoll. Here the pups worked over their mother with an enthusiasm which would certainly have driven any human female into hysterics. They were hungry; but they were also full to the ears with hellery. Two of them did their best to chew off Angeline's tail, worrying it and fighting over it until I thought I could actually see her fur flying like spindrift; while the other two did what they could to remove her ears.

Angeline stood it with noble stoicism for about an hour and then, sadly disheveled, she attempted to protect herself by sitting on her tail and tucking her mauled head down between her legs. This was a fruitless effort. The pups went for her feet, one to each paw, and I was treated to the spectacle of the demon killer of the wilds trying desperately to cover her paws, her tail, and her head at one and the same instant.

Eventually she gave it up. Harassed beyond endurance she leaped away from her brood and raced to the top of a high sand ridge behind the den. The four pups rolled cheerfully off in pursuit, but before they could reach her she gave vent to a most peculiar cry.

The whole question of wolf communications was to intrigue me more and more as time went on, but on this occasion I was still laboring under the delusion that complex communications among animals other than man did not exist. I could make nothing definite of Angeline's high-pitched and yearning whine-cum-howl. I did, however, detect a plaintive quality in it which made my sympathies go out to her.

I was not alone. Within seconds of her *cri-de-coeur*, and before the mob of pups could reach her, a savior appeared.

It was the third wolf. He had been sleeping in a bed hollowed in the sand at the southern end of the esker where it dipped down to disappear beneath the waters of the bay. I had not known he was there until I saw his head come up. He jumped to his feet, shook himself, and trotted straight toward the den—intercepting the pups as they prepared to scale the last slope to reach their mother.

I watched, fascinated, as he used his shoulder to

bowl the leading pup over on its back and send it skidding down the lower slope toward the den. Having broken the charge, he then nipped another pup lightly on its fat behind; then he shepherded the lot of them back to what I later came to recognize as the playground area.

I hesitate to put human words into a wolf's mouth, but the effect of what followed was crystal clear. "If it's a workout you kids want," he might have said, "then I'm your wolf!"

And so he was. For the next hour he played with the pups with as much energy as if he were still one himself. The games were varied, but many of them were quite recognizable. Tag was the standby, and Albert was always "it." Leaping, rolling and weaving amongst the pups, he never left the area of the nursery knoll, while at the same time leading the youngsters such a chase that they eventually gave up.

Albert looked them over for a moment and then, after a quick glance toward the crest where Angeline was now lying in a state of peaceful relaxation, he flung himself in among the tired pups, sprawled on his back, and invited mayhem. They were game. One by one they roused and went into battle. They were really roused this time, and no holds were barred—by them, at any rate.

Some of them tried to choke the life out of Albert, although their small teeth, sharp as they were, could never have penetrated his heavy ruff. One of them, in an excess of infantile sadism, turned its back on him and pawed a shower of sand into his face. The others took to leaping as high into the air as their bowed little legs would propel them; coming down with a satisfying thump on Albert's vulnerable belly. In between jumps they tried to chew the life out of whatever vulnerable parts came to tooth.

I began to wonder how much he could stand. Evidently he could stand a lot, for not until the pups were totally exhausted and had collapsed into complete somnolence did he get to his feet, careful not to step on the small, sprawled forms, and disengage himself. Even then he did not return to the comfort of his own bed (which he had undoubtedly earned after a night of hard hunting) but settled himself instead on the edge of the nursery knoll, where he began wolf-napping, taking a quick look at the pups every few minutes to make sure they were still safely near at hand.

His true relationship to the rest of the family was still uncertain; but as far as I was concerned he had become, and would remain, "good old Uncle Albert."

10

Of Mice and Wolves

AFTER SOME WEEKS of study I still seemed to be as far as ever from solving the salient problem of how the wolves made a living. This was a vital problem, since solving it in a way satisfactory to my employers was the reason for my expedition.

Caribou are the only large herbivores to be found in any numbers in the arctic Barren Lands. Although once as numerous as the plains buffalo, they had shown a catastrophic decrease during the three or four decades preceding my trip to the Barrens. Evidence obtained by various Government agencies from hunters, trappers and traders seemed to prove that the plunge of the caribou toward extinction was primarily due to the depredations of the wolf. It therefore must have seemed a safe bet, to the politicians-cum-scientists who had employed me, that a research study of wolf-caribou relationships in the Barrens would uncover incontrovertible proof with which to damn the wolf wherever he might be found, and provide a more than sufficient excuse for the adoption of a general campaign for his extirpation.

I did my duty, but although I had searched diligently for evidence which would please my superiors, I had so far found none. Nor did it appear I was likely to.

Toward the end of June, the last of the migrating caribou herds had passed Wolf House Bay heading for the high Barrens some two or three hundred miles to the north, where they would spend the summer.

Whatever my wolves were going to eat during those long months, and whatever they were going to feed their hungry pups, it would not be caribou, for the caribou were gone. But if not caribou, what *was* it to be?

I canvassed all the other possibilities I could think of, but there seemed to be no source of food available which would be adequate to satisfy the appetites of three adult and four young wolves. Apart from myself (and the thought recurred several times) there was hardly an animal left in the country which could be considered suitable prey for a wolf. Arctic hares were present; but they were very scarce and so fleet of foot that a wolf could not hope to catch one unless he was extremely lucky. Ptarmigan and other birds were numerous; but they could fly, and the wolves could not. Lake trout, arctic grayling and whitefish filled the lakes and rivers; but wolves are not otters.

The days passed and the mystery deepened. To make the problem even more inscrutable, the wolves seemed reasonably well fed; and to baffle me to the point of near insanity, the two male wolves went off hunting every night and returned every morning, but never appeared to bring anything home.

As far as I could tell, the whole lot of them seemed to be existing on a diet of air and water. Once, moved by a growing concern for their well-being, I went back to the cabin and baked five loaves of bread, which I then took to Wolf House Bay and left beside one of the hunting paths. My gift was rejected. It was even scorned. Or perhaps Uncle Albert, who discovered them, simply thought the loaves were some new sort of boundary posts which I had erected, and that they were to be treated accordingly.

About this time I began having trouble with mice. The vast expanses of spongy sphagnum bog provided

an ideal milieu for several species of small rodents
who could burrow and nest-build to their hearts'
content in the ready-made mattress of moss.

They did other things too, and they must have
done them with great frequency, for as June waned
into July the country seemed to become alive with
little rodents. The most numerous species were the
lemmings, which are famed in literature for their
reputedly suicidal instincts, but which, instead, *ought*
to be hymned for their unbelievable reproductive
capabilities. Red-backed mice and meadow mice began invading Mike's cabin in such numbers that it
looked as if *I* would soon be starving unless I could
thwart their appetites for my supplies. *They* did not
scorn my bread. They did not scorn my bed, either;
and when I awoke one morning to find that a meadow
mouse had given birth to eleven naked offspring inside the pillow of my sleeping bag, I began to know
how Pharaoh must have felt when he
antagonized the God of the Israelites.

I suppose it was only because my own wolf indoc-
trination had been so complete, and of such a stag-
geringly inaccurate nature, that it took me so long
to account for the healthy state of the wolves in the
apparent absence of any game worthy of their reputation and physical abilities. The idea of wolves not
only eating, but actually thriving and raising their
families on a diet of mice was so at odds with the
character of the mythical wolf that it was really too
ludicrous to consider. And yet, it was the answer
to the problem of how my wolves were keeping the
larder full.

Angeline tipped me off.

Late one afternoon, while the male wolves were
still resting in preparation for the night's labors, she
emerged from the den and nuzzled Uncle Albert until he yawned, stretched and got laboriously to his
feet. Then she left the den site at a trot, heading
directly for me across a broad expanse of grassy

muskeg, and leaving Albert to entertain the pups as
best he could.

There was nothing particularly new in this. I had
several times seen her conscript Albert (and on rare
occasions even George) to do duty as a babysitter
while she went down to the bay for a drink or, as I
mistakenly thought, simply went for a walk to stretch
her legs. Usually her peregrinations took her to the
point of the bay farthest from my tent where she
was hidden from sight by a low gravel ridge; but this
time she came my way in full view and so I swung
my telescope to keep an eye on her.

She went directly to the rocky foreshore, waded out
until the icy water was up to her shoulders, and had
a long drink. As she was doing so, a small flock of
Old Squaw ducks flew around the point of the Bay
and pitched only a hundred yards or so away from
her. She raised her head and eyed them speculatively
for a moment, then waded back to shore, where she
proceeded to act as if she had suddenly become
demented.

Yipping like a puppy, she began to chase her tail;
to roll over and over among the rocks; to lie on her
back; to wave all four feet furiously in the air; and in
general to behave as if she were clean out of her
mind.

I swung the glasses back to where Albert was sitting amidst a gaggle of pups to see if he, too, had
observed this mad display, and, if so, what his reaction to it was. He had seen it all right, in fact he was
watching Angeline with keen interest but without
the slightest indication of alarm.

By this time Angeline appeared to be in the throes
of a manic paroxysm, leaping wildly into the air
and snapping at nothing, the while uttering shrill
squeals. It was an awe-inspiring sight, and I
realized that Albert and I were not the only ones who
were watching it with fascination. The ducks seemed

hypnotized by curiosity. So interested were they that they swam in for a closer view of this apparition on the shore. Closer and closer they came, necks outstretched, and gabbling incredulously among themselves. And the closer they came, the crazier grew Angeline's behavior.

When the leading duck was not more than fifteen feet from shore, Angeline gave one gigantic leap towards it. There was a vast splash, a panic-stricken whacking of wings, and then all the ducks were up and away. Angeline had missed a dinner by no more than inches.

This incident was an eye-opener since it suggested a versatility at food-getting which I would hardly have credited to a human being, let alone to a mere wolf. However, Angeline soon demonstrated that the charming of ducks was a mere side line.

Having dried herself with a series of energetic shakes which momentarily hid her in a blue mist of water droplets, she padded back across the grassy swale. But now her movements were quite different from what they had been when she passed through the swale on the way to the bay.

Angeline was of a rangy build, anyway, but by stretching herself so that she literally seemed to be walking on tiptoe, and by elevating her neck like a camel, she seemed to gain several inches in height. She began to move infinitely slowly upwind across the swale, and I had the impression that both ears were cocked for the faintest sound, while I could see her nose wrinkling as she sifted the breeze for the most ephemeral scents.

Suddenly she pounced. Flinging herself up on her hind legs like a horse trying to throw its rider, she came down again with driving force, both forelegs held stiffly out in front of her. Instantly her head dropped; she snapped once, swallowed, and returned to her peculiar mincing ballet across the swale. Six times in ten minutes she repeated the straight-armed pounce, and six times she swallowed—without my having caught a glimpse of what it was that she had eaten. The seventh time she missed her aim, spun around, and began snapping frenziedly in a tangle of cotton grasses. This time when she raised her head I saw, quite unmistakably, the tail and hind quarters of a mouse quivering in her jaws. One gulp, and it too was gone.

Although I was much entertained by the spectacle of one of this continent's most powerful carnivores hunting mice, I did not really take it seriously. I thought Angeline was only having fun; snacking, as it were. But when she had eaten some twenty-three mice I began to wonder. Mice are small, but twenty-three of them adds up to a fair-sized meal, even for a wolf.

It was only later, by putting two and two together, that I was able to bring myself to an acceptance of the obvious. The wolves of Wolf House Bay, and, by inference at least, all the Barren Land wolves who were raising families outside the summer caribou range, were living largely, if not almost entirely, on mice.

Only one point remained obscure, and that was how they transported the catch of mice (which in the course of an entire night must have amounted to a formidable number of individuals) back to the dens to feed the pups. I never did solve this problem until I met some of Mike's relations. One of them, a charming fellow named Ootek, who became a close friend (and who was a first-rate, if untrained, naturalist), explained the mystery.

Since it was impossible for the wolves to carry the mice home externally, they did the next best thing and brought them home in their bellies. I had already noticed that when either George or Albert returned from a hunt they went straight to the den and crawled into it. Though I did not suspect it at the time, they were regurgitating the day's rations, already partially digested.

Later in the summer, when the pups had abandoned the den in the esker, I several times saw one of the adult wolves regurgitating a meal for them. However, if I had not known what they were doing I probably would have misconstrued the action and still been no whit the wiser as to how the wolves carried home their spoils.

The discovery that mice constituted the major item in the wolves' diet gave me a new interest in the mice themselves. I at once began a mouse-survey. The preliminary operation consisted of setting some hundred and fifty mousetraps in a nearby bog in order to obtain a representative sample of the mouse population in terms of sex, age, density and species. I chose an area of bog not far from my tent, on the theory that it would be typical of one of the bogs hunted over by the wolves, and also because it was close at hand and would therefore allow me to tend my traps frequently. This choice was a mistake. The second day my trap line was set, George happened in that direction.

I saw him coming and was undecided what to do. Since we were still scrupulously observing our mutual boundaries, I did not feel like dashing outside my enclave in an effort to head him off. On the other hand, I had no idea how he would react when he discovered that I had been poaching on his preserves.

When he reached the edge of the bog he snuffed about for a while, then cast a suspicious glance in my direction. Obviously he knew I had been trespassing but was at a loss to understand why. Making no attempt to hunt, he began walking through the cotton grass at the edge of the bog and I saw, to my horror, that he was heading straight for a cluster of ten traps set near the burrows of a lemming colony.

I had an instant flash of foreknowledge of what was going to happen, and without thought I leaped to my feet and yelled at the top of my voice:

"George! For God's sake HOLD IT!"

It was too late. My shout only startled him and he broke into a trot. He went about ten paces on the level and then he began climbing an unseen ladder to the skies.

When, sometime later, I went over to examine the site, I found he had scored six traps out of the possible ten. They could have done him no real harm, of course, but the shock and pain of having a number of his toes nipped simultaneously by an unknown antagonist must have been considerable. For the first and only time that I knew him, George lost his dignity. Yipping like a dog who has caught his tail in a door, he streaked for home, shedding mousetraps like confetti as he went.

I felt very badly about the incident. It might easily have resulted in a serious rupture in our relations. That it did not do so I can only attribute to the fact that George's sense of humor, which was well developed, led him to accept the affair as a crude practical joke—of the kind to be expected from a human being.

11

Souris à la Crême

THE REALIZATION that the wolves' summer diet
consisted chiefly of mice did not conclude my work
in the field of diatetics. I knew that the mouse-wolf
relationship was a revolutionary one to science and
would be treated with suspicion, and possibly with
ridicule, unless it could be so thoroughly
substantiated that there would be no room to doubt
its validity.

I had already established two major points:

1. That wolves caught and ate mice.

2. That the small rodents were sufficiently
   numerous to support the wolf population.

There remained, however, a third point vital to the
proof of my contention. This concerned the nutritional value of mice. It was imperative for me to
prove that a diet of small rodents would suffice
to maintain a large carnivore in good condition.

I recognized that this was not going to be an easy
task. Only a controlled experiment would do, and
since I could not exert the necessary control over the
wolves, I was at a loss how to proceed. Had Mike
still been in the vicinity I might have borrowed two
of his Huskies and, by feeding one of them on mice
alone and the other on caribou meat (if and when
this became obtainable), and then subjecting both

dogs to similar tests, I would have been able to adduce the proof for or against the validity of the mouse-wolf concept. But Mike was gone, and I had no idea when he might return.

For some days I pondered the problem, and then one morning, while I was preparing some lemmings and meadow mice as specimens, inspiration struck me. Despite the fact that man is not wholly carnivorous, I could see no valid reason why I should not use myself as a test subject. It was true that there was only one of me; but the difficulty this posed could be met by setting up two timed intervals, during one of which I would confine myself to a mouse diet while during a second period of equal length I would eat canned meat and fresh fish. At the end of each period I would run a series of physiological tests upon myself and finally compare the two sets of results. While not absolutely conclusive as far as wolves were concerned, evidence that *my* metabolic functions remained unimpaired under a mouse regimen would strongly indicate that wolves, too, could survive and function normally on the same diet.

There being no time like the present, I resolved to begin the experiment at once. Having cleaned the basinful of small corpses which remained from my morning session of mouse skinning, I placed them in a pot and hung it over my primus stove. The pot gave off a most delicate and delicious odor as the water boiled, and I was in excellent appetite by the time the stew was done.

Eating these small mammals presented something of a problem at first because of the numerous minute bones; however, I found that the bones could be chewed and swallowed without much difficulty. The taste of the mice—a purely subjective factor and not in the least relevant to the experiment—was pleasing, if rather bland. As the experiment progressed, this blandness led to a degree of boredom and a consequent loss of appetite and I was forced to seek variety in my methods of preparation.

Of the several recipes which I developed, the finest by far was Creamed Mouse, and in the event that any of my readers may be interested in personally exploiting this hitherto overlooked source of excellent animal protein, I give the recipe in full.

Souris à la Crême

Ingredients:

One dozen fat mice	Salt and pepper
One cup white flour	Cloves
One piece sowbelly	Ethyl alcohol

[I should perhaps note that sowbelly is normally only available in the arctic, but ordinary salt pork can be substituted.]

Skin and gut the mice, but do not remove the heads; wash, then place in a pot with enough alcohol to cover the carcasses. Allow to marinate for about two hours. Cut sowbelly into small cubes and fry slowly until most of the fat has been rendered. Now remove the carcasses from the alcohol and roll them in a mixture of salt, pepper and flour; then place in frying pan and sauté for about five minutes (being careful not to allow the pan to get too hot, or the delicate meat will dry out and become tough and stringy). Now add a cup of alcohol and six or eight cloves. Cover the pan and allow to simmer slowly for fifteen minutes. The cream sauce can be made according to any standard recipe. When the sauce is ready, drench the carcasses with it, cover and allow to rest in a warm place for ten minutes before serving.

During the first week of the mouse diet I found that my vigor remained unimpaired, and that I suffered no apparent ill effects. However, I did begin to develop a craving for fats. It was this which made me realize that my experiment, up to this point, had been rendered partly invalid by an over-sight—and one, moreover, which did my scientific training no credit. The wolves, as I should have remembered, *ate the whole mouse*; and my dissections had shown that these small rodents stored most of their fat in the abdominal cavity, adhering to the intestinal mesenteries, rather than subcutaneously or in the muscular tissue. It was an inexcusable error I had made, and I hastened to rectify it. From this time to the end of the experimental period I too ate the whole mouse, without the skin of course, and I found that my fat craving was considerably eased.

It was during the final stages of my mouse diet that Mike returned to his cabin. He brought with him a cousin of his, the young Eskimo, Ootek, who was to become my boon companion and who was to prove invaluable to me in my wolf researches. However, on my first encounter with Ootek I found him almost as reserved and difficult of approach as Mike had been, and in fact still remained.

I had made a trip back to the cabin to fetch some additional supplies and the sight of smoke rising from the chimney cheered me greatly, for, to tell the truth, there had been times when I would have enjoyed a little human companionship. When I entered the cabin Mike was frying a panful of ven-ison steak, while Ootek looked on. They had been lucky enough to kill a stray animal some sixty miles to the north. After a somewhat awkward few minutes, during which Mike seemed to be hopefully trying to ignore my existence, I managed to break the ice and achieve an introduction to Ootek, who responded by sliding around to the other side of the table and putting as much distance between us as possible. These two then sat down to their dinner, and Mike eventually offered me a plate of fried steak too.

I would have enjoyed eating it, but I was still conducting my experiment, and so I had to refuse, after having first explained my reasons to Mike. He accepted my excuses with the inscrutable silence of his Eskimo ancestors, but he evidently passed on my explanation to Ootek, who, whatever he may have thought about it and me, reacted in a typical Eskimoan way. Late that evening when I was about to return to my observation tent, Ootek waylaid me outside the cabin. With a shy but charming smile he held out a small parcel wrapped in deerskin. Graciously I undid the sinew binding and examined the present; for such it was. It consisted of a clutch of five small blue eggs, undoubtedly belonging to one of the thrush species, though I could not be certain of the identification.

Grateful, but at a loss to understand the implications of the gift, I returned to the cabin and asked Mike.

"Eskimo thinks if man eat mice his parts get small like mice," he explained reluctantly. "But if man eat eggs everything comes out all right. Ootek soared for you."

I was in no position—lacking sufficient evidence —to know whether or not this was a mere superstition, but there is never any harm in taking precautions. Reasoning that the eggs (which weighed less than an ounce in toto) could not affect the validity of my mouse experiment, I broke them into a frying pan and made a minute omelette. The nesting season was well advanced by this time, and so were the eggs, but I ate them anyway and, since Ootek was watching keenly, I showed every evidence of relishing them.

Delight and relief were written large upon the broad and now smiling face of the Eskimo, who was probably convinced that he had saved me from a fate worse than death.

Though I never did manage to make Mike understand the importance and nature of my scientific work, I had no such difficulty with Ootek. Or rather, perhaps I should say that though he may not have understood it, he seemed from the first to share my conviction that it *was* important. Much later I discovered that Ootek was a minor shaman, or magic priest, in his own tribe; and he had assumed, from the tales told him by Mike and from what he saw with his own eyes, that I must be a shaman too; if of a somewhat unfamiliar variety. From his point of view this assumption provided an adequate explanation for most of my otherwise inexplicable activities, and it is just possible—though I hesitate to attribute any such selfish motives to Ootek—that by associating with me he hoped to enlarge his own knowledge of the esoteric practices of his vocation.

In any event, Ootek decided to attach himself to me; and the very next day he appeared at the wolf observation tent bringing with him his sleeping robe, and obviously prepared for a long visit. My fears that he would prove to be an encumbrance and a nuisance were soon dispelled. Ootek had been taught a few words of English by Mike, and his perceptivity was so excellent that we were soon able to establish rudimentary communications. He showed no surprise when he understood that I was devoting my time to studying wolves. In fact, he conveyed to me the information that he too was keenly interested in wolves, partly because his personal totem, or helping spirit, was Amarok, the Wolf Being.

Ootek turned out to be a tremendous help. He had none of the misconceptions about wolves which, taken en masse, comprise the body of accepted writ in our society. In fact he was so close to the beasts that he considered them his actual relations. Later, when I had learned some of his language and he had improved in his knowledge of mine, he told me that as a child of about five years he had been taken to a wolf den by his father, a shaman of repute, and had been left there for twenty-four hours, during which time he made friends with and played on terms of equality with the wolf pups, and was sniffed at but otherwise unmolested by the adult wolves.

It would have been unscientific for me to have accepted all the things he told me about wolves without auxiliary proof, but I found that when such proof was obtainable he was invariably right.

12

Spirit of the Wolf

Ootek's acceptance of me had an ameliorating effect upon Mike's attitude. Although Mike continued to harbor a deep-rooted suspicion that I was not quite right in the head and might yet prove dangerous unless closely watched, he loosened up as much as his taciturn nature would permit and tried to be co-operative. This was a great boon to me, for I was able to enlist his aid as an interpreter between Ootek and myself.

Ootek had a great deal to add to my knowledge of wolves' food habits. Having confirmed what I had already discovered about the role mice played in their diet, he told me that wolves also ate great numbers of ground squirrels and at times even seemed to prefer them to caribou.

These ground squirrels are abundant throughout most of the arctic, although Wolf House Bay lies just south of their range. They are close relatives of the common gopher of the western plains, but unlike the gopher they have a very poor sense of self-preservation. Consequently they fall easy prey to wolves and foxes. In summer, when they are well fed and fat, they may weigh as much as two pounds, so that a wolf can often kill enough of them to make a good meal with only a fraction of the energy expenditure involved in hunting caribou.

I had assumed that fishes could hardly enter largely into the wolves' diet, but Ootek assured me I was wrong. He told me he had several times watched wolves fishing for jackfish or Northern pike. At spawning time in the spring these big fish, which sometimes weigh as much as forty pounds, invade the intricate network of narrow channels in boggy marshes along the lake shores.

When a wolf decides to go after them he jumps into one of the larger channels and wades upstream, splashing mightily as he goes, and driving the pike ahead of him into progressively narrower and shallower channels. Eventually the fish realizes its danger and turns to make a dash for open water; but the wolf stands in its way and one quick chop of those great jaws is enough to break the back of even the largest pike. Ootek told me he once watched a wolf catch seven large pike in less than an hour.

Wolves also caught suckers when these sluggish fish were making their spawning runs up the tundra streams, he said; but the wolf's technique in this case was to crouch on a rock in a shallow section of the stream and snatch up the suckers as they passed— a method rather similar to that employed by bears when they are catching salmon.

Another although minor source of food consisted of arctic sculpins: small fishes which lurk under rocks in shoal water. The wolves caught these by wading along the shore and turning over the rocks with paws or nose, snapping up the exposed sculpins before they could escape.

Later in the summer I was able to confirm Ootek's account of the sculpin fishery when I watched Uncle Albert spend part of an afternoon engaged in it. Unfortunately, I never did see wolves catch pike; but, having heard how they did it from Ootek, I tried it myself with considerable success, imitating the reported actions of the wolves in all respects, except that I used a short spear, instead of my teeth, with which to administer the *coup de grâce*.

These sidelights on the lupine character were fascinating, but it was when we came to a discussion of the role played by caribou in the life of the wolf that Ootek really opened my eyes.

The wolf and the caribou were so closely linked, he told me, that they were almost a single entity. He explained what he meant by telling me a story which sounded a little like something out of the Old Testament; but which, so Mike assured me, was a part of the semi-religious folklore of the inland Eskimos, who, alas for their immortal souls, were still happily heathen.

Here, paraphrased, is Ootek's tale.

"In the beginning there was a Woman and a Man, and nothing else walked or swam or flew in the world until one day the Woman dug a great hole in the ground and began fishing in it. One by one she pulled out all the animals, and the last one she pulled out of the hole was the caribou. Then Kaila, who is the God of the Sky, told the woman the caribou was the greatest gift of all, for the caribou would be the sustenance of man.

"The Woman set the caribou free and ordered it to go out over the land and multiply, and the caribou did as the Woman said; and in time the land was filled with caribou, so the sons of the Woman hunted well, and they were fed and clothed and had good skin tents to live in, all from the caribou.

"The sons of the Woman hunted only the big, fat caribou, for they had no wish to kill the weak and the small and the sick, since these were no good to eat nor were their skins much good. And, after a time, it happened that the sick and the weak came to outnumber the fat and the strong, and when the sons saw this they were dismayed and they complained to the Woman.

"Then the Woman made magic and spoke to Kaila and said: 'Your work is no good, for the caribou grow weak and sick, and if we eat them we must grow weak and sick also.'

"Kaila heard, and he said 'My work is good. I shall tell Amorak [the spirit of the Wolf], and he shall tell his children, and they will eat the sick and the weak and the small caribou, so that the land will be left for the fat and the good ones.'

"And this is what happened, and this is why the caribou and the wolf are one; for the caribou feeds the wolf, but it is the wolf who keeps the caribou strong."

I was slightly stunned by this story, for I was not prepared to have an unlettered and untutored Eskimo give me a lecture, even in parable form, illustrating the theory of survival of the fittest through the agency of natural selection. In any event, I was skeptical about the happy relationship which Ootek postulated as existing between caribou and wolf. Although I had already been disabused of the truth of a good many scientifically established beliefs about wolves by my own recent experiences, I could hardly believe that the all-powerful and intelligent wolf would limit his predation on the caribou herds to culling the sick and the infirm when he could, presumably, take his choice of the fattest and most succulent individuals. Furthermore, I had what I thought was excellent ammunition with which to demolish Ootek's thesis.

"Ask him then," I told Mike, "how come there are so many skeletons of big and evidently healthy caribou scattered around the cabin and all over the tundra for miles to the north of here."

"Don't need to ask him that," Mike replied with unabashed candor. "It was me killed those deer. I got fourteen dogs to feed and it takes maybe two, three caribou a week for that. I got to feed myself too. And then, I got to kill lots of deer everywhere all over the trapping country. I set four, five traps around each deer like that and get plenty foxes when they come to feed. It is no use for me to shoot skinny caribou. What I got to have is the big fat ones."

I was staggered. "How many do you think you kill in a year?" I asked.

Mike grinned proudly. "I'm pretty damn good shot. Kill maybe two, three hundred, maybe more."

When I had partially recovered from that one, I asked him if this was the usual thing for trappers.

"Every trapper got to do the same," he said. "Indians, white men, all the way down south far as caribou go in the wintertime, they got to kill lots of them or they can't trap no good. Of course they not all the time lucky to get *enough* caribou; then they got to feed the dogs on fish. But dogs can't work good on fish—get weak and sick and can't haul no loads. Caribou is better."

I knew from having studied the files at Ottawa that there were eighteen hundred trappers in those portions of Saskatchewan, Manitoba, and southern Keewatin which composed the winter range of the Keewatin caribou herd. I also knew that many of these trappers had been polled by Ottawa, through the agency of the fur trading companies, for information which might help explain the rapid decline in the size of the Keewatin caribou herd. I had read the results of this poll. To a man, the trappers and traders denied that they killed more than one or two caribou a year; and to a man they had insisted that wolves slaughtered the deer in untold thousands.

Although mathematics have never been my strong point, I tried to work out some totals from the information at hand. Being a naturally conservative fellow, I cut the number of trappers in half, and then cut Mike's annual caribou kill in half, before multiplying the two. No matter how many times I multiplied, I kept coming up with the fantastic figure of 112,000 animals killed by trappers in this area every year.

I realized it was not a figure I could use in my reports—not unless I wished to be posted to the Galapagos Islands to conduct a ten-year study on tortoise ticks.

In any event, what Mike and Ootek had told me was largely hearsay evidence, and this was not what I was employed to gather. Resolutely I put these disturbing revelations out of mind, and went back to learning the truth the hard way.

13

Wolf Talk

OOTEK HAD many singular attributes as a naturalist, not the least of which was his apparent ability to understand wolf language.

Before I met Ootek I had already noted that the variety and range of the vocal noises made by George, Angeline and Uncle Albert far surpassed the ability of any other animals I knew about save man alone. In my notebooks I had recorded the following categories of sounds: Howls, wails, quavers, whines, grunts, growls, yips and barks. Within each of these categories I had recognized, but had been unable adequately to describe, innumerable variations. I was also aware that canines in general are able to hear, and presumably to make, noises both above and below the range of human registry; the so-called "soundless" dog-whistle which is commercially available being a case in point. I knew too that individual wolves from my family group appeared to react in an intelligent manner to sounds made by other wolves, although I had no certain evidence that these sounds were anything more than simple signals.

My real education in lupine linguistics began a few days after Ootek's arrival. The two of us had been observing the wolf den for several hours without seeing anything of note. It was a dead-calm day, so that the flies had reached plague proportions, and Angeline and the pups had retired to the den to escape while both males, exhausted after a hunt which had lasted into mid-morning, were sleeping nearby. I was getting bored and sleepy myself when

Ootek suddenly cupped his hands to his ears and began to listen intently.

I could hear nothing, and I had no idea what had caught his attention until he said: "Listen, the wolves are talking!" and pointed toward a range of hills some five miles to the north of us.*

I listened, but if a wolf was broadcasting from those hills he was not on my wavelength. I heard nothing except the baleful buzzing of mosquitoes; but George, who had been sleeping on the crest of the esker, suddenly sat up, cocked his ears forward and pointed his long muzzle toward the north. After a minute or two he threw back his head and howled; a long, quavering howl which started low and ended on the highest note my ears would register.

Ootek grabbed my arm and broke into a delighted grin.

"Caribou are coming; the wolf says so!"

I got the gist of this, but not much more than the gist, and it was not until we returned to the cabin and I again had Mike's services as an interpreter that I learned the full story.

According to Ootek, a wolf living in the next territory to the north had not only informed our wolves that the long-awaited caribou had started to move south, but had even indicated where they were at the moment. To make the story even more improbable, this wolf had not actually seen the caribou himself, but had simply been passing on a report received from a still more distant wolf. George, having heard and understood, had then passed on the good news in his turn.

I am incredulous by nature and by training, and I

---

*During the two-year period that I knew Ootek, his English improved considerably, and I learned quite a lot of Eskimo, so that we were able to converse freely. I have therefore converted our earlier conversations, which tended to be complicated, into a form more understandable to the reader.

made no secret of my amusement at the naïveté of Ootek's attempt to impress me with this fantastic yarn. But if I was incredulous, Mike was not. Without more ado he began packing up for a hunting trip.

I was not surprised at his anxiety to kill a deer, for I had learned one truth by now, that he, as well as every other human being on the Barrens, was a meat eater who lived almost exclusively on caribou when they were available; but I *was* amazed that he should be willing to make a two- or three-day hike over the tundra on evidence as wild as that which Ootek offered. I said as much, but Mike went taciturn and left without another word.

Three days later, when I saw him again, he offered me a haunch of venison and a pot of caribou tongues. He also told me he had found the caribou exactly where Ootek, interpreting the wolf message, had said they would be—on the shores of a lake called Kooiak some forty miles northeast of the cabin.

I knew this *had* to be coincidence. But being curious as to how far Mike would go, to pull my leg, I feigned conversion and asked him to tell me more about Ootek's uncanny skill.

Mike obliged. He explained that the wolves not only possessed the ability to communicate over great distances but, so he insisted, could "talk" almost as well as we could. He admitted that he himself could neither hear all the sounds they made, nor understand most of them, but he said some Eskimos, and Ootek in particular, could hear and understand so well that they could quite literally converse with wolves.

I mulled this information over for a while and concluded that anything this pair told me from then on would have to be recorded with a heavy sprinkling of question marks.

However, the niggling idea kept recurring that there just *might* be something in it all, so I asked

Mike to tell Ootek to keep track of what our wolves said in future, and, through Mike, to keep me informed.

The next morning when we arrived at the den there was no sign of either of the male wolves. Angeline and the pups were up and about, but Angeline seemed ill at ease. She kept making short trips to the crest of the den ridge, where she stood in a listening attitude for a few minutes before returning to the pups. Time passed, and George and Uncle Albert were considerably overdue. Then, on her fifth trip to the ridge, Angeline appeared to hear something. So did Ootek. Once more he went through his theatrical performance of cupping both ears. After listening a moment he proceeded to try to give me an explanation of what was going on. Alas, we were not yet sufficiently en rapport, and this time I did not even get the gist of what he was saying.

I went back to my observing routine, while Ootek crawled into the tent for a sleep. I noted in my log that George and Uncle Albert arrived back at the den together, obviously exhausted, at 12:17 P.M. About 2:00 P.M. Ootek woke up and made amends for his dereliction of duty by brewing me a pot of tea.

The next time we encountered Mike I recalled him to his promise and he began to interrogate Ootek.

"Yesterday," he told me, "Ootek says that wolf you call George, he send a message to his wife. Ootek hear it good. He tell his wife the hunting is pretty bad and he going to stay out longer. Maybe not get home until the middle of the day."

I remembered that Ootek could not have known at what time the male wolves returned home, for he was then fast asleep *inside* the tent. And 12:17 is close enough to the middle of the day for any practical purpose.

Nevertheless, for two more days my skepticism ruled—until the afternoon when once again George appeared on the crest and cocked his ears toward the north. Whatever he heard, if he heard anything, did not seem to interest him much this time, for he did not howl, but went off to the den to sniff noses with Angeline.

Ootek, on the other hand, was definitely interested. Excitement filled his face. He fairly gabbled at me, but I caught only a few words. *Innuit* (eskimos) and *kiyai* (come) were repeated several times, as he tried passionately to make me understand. When I still looked dense he gave me an exasperated glance and, without so much as a by-your-leave, headed off across the tundra in a direction which would have taken him to the northwest of Mike's cabin.

I was a little annoyed by his cavalier departure, but I soon forgot about it, for it was now late afternoon and all the wolves were becoming restless as the time approached for the males to set off on the evening hunt.

There was a definite ritual about these preparations. George usually began them by making a visit to the den. If Angeline and the pups were inside, his visit brought them out. If they were already outside, Angeline's behavior changed from that of domestic boredom to one of excitement. She would begin to romp; leaping in front of George, charging him with her shoulder, and embracing him with her forelegs. George seemed at his most amiable during these playful moments, and would sometimes respond by engaging in a mock battle with his mate. From where I sat these battles looked rather ferocious, but the steadily wagging tails of both wolves showed it was all well meant.

No doubt alerted by the sounds of play, Uncle Albert would appear on the scene and join the group. He often chose to sleep away the daylight hours some distance from the den site, perhaps in order to reduce the possibility of being dragooned into the role of babysitter at too frequent intervals.

With his arrival, all three adult wolves would stand in a circle, sniff noses, wag their tails hard, and make noises. "Make noises" is not very descriptive, but it is the best I can do. I was too far off to hear more than the louder sounds, and these appeared to be more like grunts than anything else. Their meaning was obscure to me, but they were certainly connected with a general feeling of good will, anticipation and high spirits.

After anywhere from twenty minutes to an hour of conviviality (in which the pups took part, getting under everyone's feet and nipping promiscuously at any adult tail they might encounter) the three adults would adjourn to the crest of the den, usually led by Angeline. Once more they would form a circle and then, lifting their heads high, would "sing" for a few minutes.

This was one of the high points of their day, and it was certainly *the* high point of mine. The first few times the three wolves sang, the old ingrained fear set my back hairs tingling, and I cannot claim to having really enjoyed the chorus. However, with the passage of sufficient time I not only came to enjoy it, but to anticipate it with acute pleasure. And yet I find it almost impossible to describe, for the only terms at my disposal are those relating to human music and these are inadequate if not actually misleading. The best I can do is to say that this full-throated and great-hearted chorus moved me as I have very occasionally been moved by the bowel-shaking throb and thunder of a superb organ played by a man who had transcended his mere manhood.

The impassionata never lasted long enough for me. In three or four minutes it would come to an end and the circle would break up; once more with much tail wagging, nose sniffing and general evidence of good will and high content. Then, reluctantly, Angeline would move toward the den, often looking back to watch as George and Albert trotted off along one of the hunting trails. She made it clear that she wished desperately to join them; but in the end she would rejoin the pups instead, and once more submit to their ebullient demands, either for dinner or for play.

On this particular night the male wolves made a break from their usual routine. Instead of taking one of the trails leading north, or northwest, they headed off toward the east, in the opposite direction from Mike's cabin and me.

I thought no more about this variation until sometime later when a human shout made me turn around. Ootek had returned—but he was not alone. With him were three bashful friends, all grinning, and all shy at this first meeting with the strange *kablunak* who was interested in wolves.

The arrival of such a mob made further observations that night likely to be unproductive, so I joined the four Eskimos in the trek to the cabin. Mike was home, and greeted the new visitors as old friends. Eventually I found a chance to ask him a few questions.

Yes, he told me, Ootek had indeed known that these men were on their way, and would soon arrive.

How did he know?

A foolish question. He knew because he had heard the wolf on the Five Mile Hills reporting the passage of the Eskimos through his territory. He had tried to tell me about it; but then, when I failed to understand, he had felt obliged to leave me in order to intercept and greet his friends.

And that was that.

14

Puppy Time

DURING THE third week in June, Angeline began to show increasing signs of restlessness. She gave the distinct impression that her too domestic life at the den was beginning to pall. When George and Albert departed of an evening for the hunt, she took to accompanying them on the first part of their journey. At first she went no further than a hundred yards from the den; but on one occasion she covered a quarter of a mile before returning slowly home.

George was clearly delighted with her changing mood. He had been trying for weeks to persuade her to join him on the night-long ranging across the tundra. On one occasion he had delayed his departure by a good hour—long after Albert had grown impatient and struck off on his own—in an attempt to entice his mate into going along.

During that hour he made eight trips from the lookout ridge down to the nursery knoll where Angeline was lying in the midst of her pups. Each time he sniffed her fondly, wagged his tail furiously and then started hopefully off toward the hunting trail. And each time, when she failed to follow, he returned to the lookout knoll to sit disconsolately for a few minutes before trying again. When he finally did depart, alone, he was the picture of disappointment and dejection, with head and tail both held so low that he seemed to slink away.

The desire to have a night out together was clearly

mutual, but the welfare of the pups remained paramount with Angeline, even though they seemed large enough and able enough to need far less attention.

On the evening of June 23 I was alone at the tent —Ootek having gone off on some business of his own for a few days—when the wolves gathered for their pre-hunt ritual singsong. Angeline surpassed herself on this occasion, lifting her voice in such an untrammeled paean of longing that I wished there were some way I could volunteer to look after the kids while she went off with George. I need not have bothered. Uncle Albert also got the message, or perhaps he had received more direct communications, for when the song was done Angeline and George trotted buoyantly off together, while Albert mooched morosely down to the den and settled himself in for an all-night siege of pups.

A few hours later a driving rain began and I had to give up my observations.

There were no wolves in sight the next morning when the rain ceased, the mist lifted, and I could again begin observing; but shortly before nine o'clock George and Uncle Albert appeared on the crest of the esker.

Both seemed nervous, or at least uneasy. After a good deal of restless pacing, nose sniffing, and short periods of immobility during which they stared intently over the surrounding landscape, they split up. George took himself off to the highest point of the esker, where he sat down in full view and began to scan the country to the east and south. Uncle Albert trotted off along the ridge to the north, and lay down on a rocky knoll, staring out over the western plains.

There was still no sign of Angeline, and this, together with the unusual actions of the male wolves, began to make me uneasy too. The thought that something might have happened to Angeline struck

me with surprising pain. I had not realized how fond
I was becoming of her, but now that she appeared
to be missing I began to worry about her in dead
earnest.

I was on the point of leaving my tent and climbing
the ridge to have a look for her myself, when she
forestalled me. As I took a last quick glance through
the telescope I saw her emerge from the den—with
something in her mouth—and start briskly across
the face of the esker. For a moment I could not
make out what it was she was carrying, then with a
start of surprise I recognized it as one of the pups.

Making good time despite her burden—the pup
must have weighed ten or fifteen pounds—she
trotted diagonally up the esker slope and disappeared
into a small stand of spruce. Fifteen minutes later
she was back at the den for another pup, and by
ten o'clock she had moved the last of them.

After she disappeared for the final time both male
wolves gave up their vigils—they had evidently
been keeping guard over the move—and followed
her, leaving me to stare bleakly over an empty landscape. I was greatly perturbed. The only explanation which I could think of for this mass exodus was
that I had somehow disturbed the wolves so seriously
they had felt impelled to abandon their den. If this
was indeed the case, I knew I would only make
matters worse by trying to follow them. Not being
able to think of anything else to do, I hurried back
to the cabin to consult Ootek.

The Eskimo immediately set my fears at rest. He
explained that this shifting of the pups was a normal
occurrence with every wolf family at about this time
of year. There were several reasons for it, so he told
me. In the first place the pups had now been
weaned, and, since there was no water supply near
the den, it was necessary to move them to a location
where they could slack their thirst elsewhere than

at their mother's teats. Secondly, the pups were growing too big for the den, which now could barely
contain them all. Thirdly, and perhaps most important, it was time for the youngsters to give up baby-
hood and begin their education.

"They are too old to live in a hole in the ground,
but still too young to follow their parents," Mike
interpreted, as Ootek explained. "So the old wolves
take them to a new place where there is room for
the pups to move around and to learn about the
world, but where they are still safe."

As it happened both Ootek and Mike were familiar
with the location of the new "summer den," and the
next day we moved the observation tent to a position partly overlooking it.

The pups' new home, half a mile from the old den,
was a narrow, truncated ravine filled with gigantic
boulders which had been split off the cliff walls by
frost action. A small stream ran through it. It also
embraced an area of grassy marsh which was alive
with meadow mice: an ideal place for the pups to
learn the first principles of hunting. Exit to and
entry from the ravine involved a stiff climb, which
was too much for the youngsters, so that they could
be left in their new home with little danger of their
straying; and since they were now big enough to
hold their own with the only other local carnivores
of any stature—the foxes and hawks—they had nothing to fear.

I decided to allow the wolves time to settle in at
the summer den before resuming my close watch
upon them, and so I spent the next night at the cabin
catching up on my notes.

That evening Ootek added several new items to
my fund of information. Among other interesting
things he told me that wolves were longer-lived than
dogs. He had personally known several wolves who

were at least sixteen years old, while one wolf patriarch who lived near the Kazan River, and who had been well known to Ootek's father, must have been over twenty years old before he disappeared.

He also told me that wolves have the same general outlook toward pups that Eskimos have toward children—which is to say that actual paternity does not count for much, and there are no orphans as we use the term.

Some years earlier a wolf bitch who was raising her family only a mile or two from the camp where Ootek was then living was shot and killed by a white man who was passing through the country by canoe. Ootek, who considered himself to be magically related to all wolves, was very upset by the incident. There was a Husky bitch with pups in the Eskimo camp at the time, and so he determined to dig out the wolf pups and put them with the bitch. However, his father deterred him by telling him it would not be necessary—that the wolves would solve the problem in their own way.

Although his father was a great shaman, and could be relied upon to speak the truth, Ootek was not wholly convinced and so he took up his own vigil over the den. He had not been in hiding many hours, so he told me, when he saw a strange wolf appear in company with the widowed male, and both wolves entered the den. When they came out, each was carrying a pup.

Ootek followed them for several miles until he realized they were heading for a second wolf den, the location of which was also known to him. By running hard, and by taking short cuts, he reached this second den before the two wolves did, and was present when they arrived.

As soon as they appeared the female who owned the den, and who had a litter of her own, came to the den mouth, seized the two pups one after another

by the scruff of their necks and took them into the
den. The two males then departed to fetch another
pair of pups.

When the move was completed there were ten
pups at this second den, all much of a size and age
and, as far as Ootek could tell, all treated with identical care and kindness by the several adults, now
including the bereaved male.

This was a touching story, but I am afraid I did
not give it due credence until some years later when
I heard of an almost identical case of adoption of
motherless wolf pups. On this occasion my informant
was a white naturalist of such repute that I could
hardly doubt his word—though, come to think of it,
I am hard put to explain just why *his* word should
have any more weight than Ootek's, who was, after
all, spiritually almost a wolf himself.

I took this opportunity to ask Ootek if he had ever
heard of the time-honored belief that wolves sometime adopt human children. He smiled at what he
evidently took to be my sense of humor, and the gist
of his reply was that this was a pretty idea, but it
went beyond the bounds of credibility. I was somewhat taken aback by his rather condescending refusal
to accept the wolf-boy as a reality, but I was really
shaken when he explained further.

A human baby put in a wolf den would die, he
said, not because the wolves wished it to die, but
simply because it would be incapable, by virtue of
its inherent helplessness, of living as a wolf. On the
other hand it was perfectly possible for a woman to
nurse a pup to healthy adulthood, and this sometimes happened in Eskimo camps when a Husky bitch
died. Furthermore, he knew of at least two occasions
where a woman who had lost her own child and was
heavy with milk had nursed a wolf pup—Husky pups
not being available at the time.

15

Uncle Albert Falls in Love

THE NEW location of the summer den was ideal from the wolves' point of view, but not from mine, for the clutter of boulders made it difficult to see what was happening. In addition, caribou were now trickling back into the country from the north, and the pleasures of the hunt were siren calls to all three adult wolves. They still spent most of each day at or near the summer den, but they were usually so tired from their nightly excursions that they did little but sleep.

I was beginning to find time hanging heavy on my hands when Uncle Albert rescued me from boredom by falling in love.

When Mike departed from the cabin shortly after my first arrival there he had taken all his dogs with him—not, as I suspected, because he did not trust them in the vicinity of my array of scalpels, but because the absence of caribou made it impossible to feed them. Throughout June his team had remained with the Eskimos, whose camps were in the caribous' summer territory; but now that the deer were returning south the Eskimo who had been keeping the dogs brought them back.

Mike's dogs were of aboriginal stock, and were magnificent beasts. Contrary to yet another myth, Eskimo dogs are not semi-domesticated wolves—though both species may well have sprung from the same ancestry. Smaller in stature than wolves, true

Huskies are of a much heavier build, with broad chests, shorter necks, and bushy tails which curl over their rumps like plumes. They differ from wolves in other ways too. Unlike their wild relations, Husky bitches come into heat at any time of the year with a gay disregard for seasons.

When Mike's team returned to the cabin one of the bitches was just coming into heat. Being hot-blooded by nature, and amorous by inclination, this particular bitch soon had the rest of the team in an uproar and was causing Mike no end of trouble. He was complaining about the problem one evening when inspiration came to me.

Because of their continent habits, my study of the wolves had so far revealed nothing about their sexual life and, unless I was prepared to follow them about during the brief mating season in March, when they would be wandering with the caribou herds, I stood no chance of filling in this vital gap in my knowledge.

Now I knew, from what Mike and Ootek had already told me, that wolves are not against miscegenation. In fact they will mate with dogs, or vice versa, whenever the opportunity arises. It does not arise often, because the dogs are almost invariably tied up except when working, but it *does* happen.

I put my proposition to Mike and to my delight he agreed. In fact he seemed quite pleased, for it appeared that he had long wished to discover for himself what kind of sled dogs a wolf-husky cross would make.

The next problem was how to arrange the experiment so that my researches would benefit to the maximum degree. I decided to do the thing in stages. The first stage was to consist of taking the bitch, whose name was Kooa, for a walk around the vicinity of my new observation site, in order to make her existence and condition known to the wolves.

Kooa was more than willing. In fact, when we

crossed one of the wolf trails she became so enthusiastic it was all I could do to restrain her impetuosity by means of a heavy chain leash. Dragging me behind her she plunged down the trail, sniffing every marker with uninhibited anticipation.

It was with great difficulty that I dragged her back to the cabin where, once she was firmly tethered, she reacted by howling her frustration the whole night through.

Or perhaps it was not frustration that made her sing; for when I got up next morning Ootek informed me we had had a visitor. Sure enough, the tracks of a big wolf were plainly visible in the wet sand of the riverbank not a hundred yards from the dog-lines. Probably it was only the presence of the jealous male Huskies which had prevented the romance from being consummated that very night.

I had been unprepared for such quick results, although I should have foreseen that either George or Albert would have been sure to find some of Kooa's seductively scented billets-doux that same evening.

I now had to rush the second phase of my plan into execution. Ootek and I repaired to the observation tent and, a hundred yards beyond it in the direction of the summer den, we strung a length of heavy wire between two rocks about fifty feet from one another.

The next morning we led Kooa (or more properly, were led *by* Kooa) to the site. Despite her determined attempts to go off wolf seeking on her own, we managed to shackle her chain to the wire. She retained considerable freedom of movement with this arrangement, and we could command her position from the tent with rifle fire in case anything went wrong.

Rather to my surprise she settled down at once and spent most of the afternoon sleeping. No adult wolves were in evidence near the summer den, but we caught glimpses of the pups occasionally as they lumbered about the little grassy patch, leaping and pouncing after mice.

About 8:30 P.M. the wolves suddenly broke into their pre-hunting song, although they themselves remained invisible behind a rock ridge to the south of the den.

The first sounds had barely reached me when Kooa leaped to her feet and joined the chorus. And *how* she howled! Although there is not, as far as I am aware, any canine or lupine blood in my veins, the seductive quality of Kooa's siren song was enough to set me thinking longingly of other days and other joys.

That the wolves understood the burden of her plaint was not long in doubt. Their song stopped in mid-swing, and seconds later all three of them came surging over the crest of the ridge into our view. Although she was a quarter of a mile away, Kooa was clearly visible to them. After only a moment's hesitation, both George and Uncle Albert started toward her at a gallop.

George did not get very far. Before he had gone fifty yards Angeline had overtaken him and, while I am not prepared to swear to this, I had the distinct impression that she somehow tripped him. At any rate he went sprawling in the muskeg, and when he picked himself up his interest in Kooa seemed to have evaporated. To do him justice, I do not believe he was interested in her in a sexual way—probably he was simply taking the lead in investigating a strange intruder into his domain. In any event, he and Angeline withdrew to the summer den, where they lay down together on the lip of the ravine and watched proceedings, leaving it up to Uncle Albert to handle the situation as he saw fit.

I do not know how long Albert had been celibate,

but it had clearly been too long. When he reached the area where Kooa was tethered he was moving so fast he overshot. For one tense moment I thought he had decided we were competing suitors and was going to continue straight on into the tent to deal with us; but he got turned somehow, and his wild rush slowed. Then when he was within ten feet of Kooa, who was awaiting his arrival in a state of ecstatic anticipation, Albert's manner suddenly changed. He stopped dead in his tracks, lowered his great head, and turned into a buffoon.

It was an embarrassing spectacle. Laying his ears back until they were flush with his broad skull, he began to wiggle like a pup while at the same time wrinkling his lips in a frightful grimace which may have been intended to register infatuation, but which looked to me more like a symptom of senile decay. He also began to whine in a wheedling falsetto which would have sounded disgusting coming from a Pekinese.

Kooa seemed nonplussed by his remarkable behavior. Obviously she had never before been wooed in this surprising manner, and she seemed uncertain what to do about it. With a half-snarl she backed away from Albert as far as her chain would permit.

This sent Albert into a frenzy of abasement. Belly to earth, he began to grovel toward her while his grimace widened into an expression of sheer idiocy.

I now began to share Kooa's concern, and thinking the wolf had taken complete leave of his senses I was about to seize the rifle and go to Kooa's rescue, when Ootek restrained me. He was grinning; a frankly salacious grin, and he was able to make it clear that I was not to worry; that things were progressing perfectly normally from a wolfish point of view.

At this point Albert shifted gears with bewildering rapidity. Scrambling to his feet he suddenly became the lordly male. His ruff expanded until it made a huge silvery aura framing his face. His body stiffened until he seemed to be made of white steel. His tail rose until it was as high, and almost as tightly curled, as a true Husky's. Then, pace by delicate pace, he closed the gap.

Kooa was no longer in doubt. *This* was something she could understand. Rather coyly she turned her back toward him and as he stretched out his great nose to offer his first caress she spun about and nipped him coyly on the shoulder. . . .

My notes on the rest of this incident are fully detailed but I fear they are too technical and full of scientific terminology to deserve a place in this book. I shall therefore content myself by summing up what followed with the observation that Albert certainly knew how to make love.

My scientific curiosity had been assuaged, but Uncle Albert's passion hadn't, and a most difficult situation now developed. Although we waited with as much patience as we could muster for two full hours, Albert showed not the slightest indication of ever intending to depart from his new-found love. Ootek and I wished to return to the cabin with Kooa, and we could not wait forever. In some desperation we finally made a sally toward the enamored pair.

Albert stood his ground, or rather he ignored us totally. Even Ootek seemed somewhat uncertain how to proceed after we reached a point not fifteen feet from the lovers without Albert's having given any sign that he might be inclined to leave. It was a stalemate which was only broken when I, with much reluctance, fired a shot into the ground a little way from where Albert stood.

The shot woke him from his trance. He leaped high into the air and bounded off a dozen yards, but having quickly recovered his equanimity he started to edge back toward us. Meanwhile we had untied the chain, and while Ootek dragged the sullenly reluctant Kooa off toward home, I covered the rear with the rifle.

Albert stayed right with us. He kept fifteen to twenty yards away, sometimes behind, sometimes on the flanks, sometimes in front; but leave us he would not.

Back at the cabin we again tried to cool his ardor by firing a volley in the air, but this had no effect except to make him withdraw a few yards farther off. There was obviously nothing for it but to take Kooa into the cabin for the night; for to have chained her on the dog-line with her teammates would have resulted in a battle royal between them and Albert.

It was a frightful night. The moment the door closed, Albert broke into a lament. He wailed and whooped and yammered without pause for hours. The dogs responded with a cacophony of shrill insults and counterwails. Kooa joined in by screaming messages of undying love. It was an intolerable situation. By morning Mike was threatening to do some more shooting, and in real earnest.

It was Ootek who saved the day, and possibly Albert's life as well. He convinced Mike that if he released Kooa, all would be well. She would not run away, he explained, but would stay in the vicinity of the camp with the wolf. When her period of heat was over she would return home and the wolf would go back to his own kind.

He was perfectly right, as usual. During the next week we sometimes caught glimpses of the lovers walking shoulder to shoulder across some distant ridge. They never went near the den esker, nor did they come close to the cabin. They lived in a world all their own, oblivious to everything except each other.

They were not aware of us, but I was uncomfortably aware of them, and I was glad when, one morning, we found Kooa lying at her old place in the dog-line looking exhausted but satiated.

The next evening Uncle Albert once more joined in the evening ritual chorus at the wolf esker. However, there was now a mellow, self-satisfied quality to his voice that I had never heard before, and it set my teeth on edge. Braggadocio is an emotion which I have never been able to tolerate—not even in wolves.

16

Morning Meat Delivery

SINCE THE removal of the pups to the ravine they had been largely hidden from my view; and so one morning, before Angeline or the two males had returned from the nightly hunt, I made my way to an outcropping of rocks crowned with a scrub of dwarfed spruces which overlooked the ravine from a distance of less than a hundred feet. There was only the faintest puff of wind and it was blowing from the northeast, so that any wolves at the den, or approaching it, would not be likely to get my scent. I settled myself among the spruces and scanned the floor of the ravine.

The entire area (an enclosure about thirty yards long by ten wide) was crisscrossed with trails. As I watched, two pups emerged from a jumble of shattered rocks under one wall of the ravine and scampered down one of the trails toward the tiny stream. They drew up alongside each other at the stream's edge and plunged their blunt little faces into the water, wagging their stubby tails the while.

They had grown a good deal in the past weeks, and were now about the size of and roughly the same shape as full-grown groundhogs. They were so fat their legs seemed dwarfed, and their woolly gray coats of puppy hair made them look even more rotund. I could see no promise in them of the lithe and magnificent physique which characterized their parents.

A third pup emerged into view a little farther down the gully, dragging with him the well-chewed scapula of a caribou. He was growling over it as if it were alive and dangerous, and the pups by the stream heard him, lifted their dripping faces, and then bounced off in his direction.

A free-for-all now developed and the air was filled with puppy growls and shrill yips of outrage as one or another of the little beasts sank his needle teeth into a brother's leg. The fourth pup appeared and flung himself into the melee with an ecstatic squeal of pleasure.

After four or five minutes of this internecine warfare a raven flew low over the gully, and as his shadow slipped past the pups they abandoned the bone and scuttled for shelter. But this was evidently only part of the game, for they emerged again at once showing no signs of real fear. While two of them went back to battling over the bone, the other two ambled off to the muskeg patch and began sniffing about for mice.

Any mice which still remained in this small area must have become exceptionally cagey. After a few minutes of perfunctory snuffling, and one or two attempts to burrow into the muck, these pups gave up the attempt to hunt and started playing with each other.

It was at this moment that Angeline returned.

I was so engrossed in watching the pups that I was not aware of her presence until I heard a deep whine near at hand. The pups heard it too, and we all swiveled our heads to see Angeline at the edge of the ravine. The pups instantly abandoned their games and set up a shrill yammer of excitement, one of them even standing up on his pudgy hindlegs and pawing the air in joyful anticipation.

Angeline watched them for a second or two, poised and lovely, then leaped over the rim and down to the valley floor, where she was mobbed. She sniffed each pup, turning some of them right over on their backs in the process, then she hunched her shoulders and began to retch.

Although I should have known what to expect, I was caught off guard and for a horrible moment was afraid she had eaten poison. Nothing of the kind. After several convulsive motions she brought up what appeared to be at least ten pounds of partly digested meat, then she leaped out of the way and lay down to watch the pups go to it.

If the morning meat delivery made me somewhat squeamish, it did not inhibit the pups. With single-minded voracity they waded into their breakfast while Angeline watched them tolerantly, making no attempt to correct their appalling manners.

Breakfast finished—and not a scrap remained for lunch—the pups simply keeled over where they stood —bloated, and evidently incapable of any further hellery for the moment.

The somnolence of a hot summer morning descended on us all. Very soon I was the only one still awake, and I was having a hard time staying that way. I would have liked to ease my position a little and have a stretch; but I did not dare move, for I was so close to the wolves and the silence was so complete that they would have heard the slightest sound I made.

It may be indelicate of me to mention it, but I seem to have been equipped at birth with the equivalent of an echo chamber in my stomach regions. When I am hungry, or even sometimes when I am not, this portion of my anatomy becomes autonomous and begins producing noises of a startling variety and volume and of a carrying power which has to be heard to be believed. There is nothing I can do about it, although, over the years I have at least learned how to mitigate the consequences by pre-

tending, with some skill, that I am not involved, and
that the rumblings which others hear do not proceed
from me.

My demon drummer of the nether depths now
chose to do his stuff, and the resultant cacophony
rolled through the hush of the morning like distant
thunder.

Angeline woke with a start. Her head went up
and she listened intently, but with a puzzled expression. When the sounds continued (despite everything I could do to muffle them) she got slowly to
her feet and, after a glance at the pups, as if to
assure herself that *they* were not responsible, she
cocked a speculative eye at the cloudless sky above.
It held no solution to the mystery. Thoroughly
aroused now, she began trying to track down the
sounds.

This was no easy task, for there is a pronounced
ventriloquial effect to abdominal noises in general
and to mine in particular. After walking up and
down the ravine twice, Angeline seemed no closer to
satisfying her mounting curiosity.

I was undecided whether to attempt a retreat or
whether to stand my ground in the hopes that my
internal orchestra would exhaust itself; but the orchestra showed that it was still full of vim and vigor
by producing a new and protracted rumble, of earth-
shaking proportions. Moments later Angeline's head
appeared over the rim of the gully about ten feet
from me.

We stared mutely into each other's eyes for several
seconds. At least *she* was mute, and I was trying
very hard to be, but with limited success. It was an
extraordinarily embarrassing predicament: the more
I had seen of Angeline, the higher my regard for her
had risen; I valued her good opinion, and I did not
want to appear foolish in her eyes.

However I may have appeared, I *felt* extremely
foolish. Her sudden appearance seemed to stimulate

my intestinal musicians to more splendid efforts, and, before I could think of any feasible way of excusing myself, Angeline wrinkled her lips, bared her superb white teeth in an expression of cold disdain, and vanished.

Hastily abandoning my hiding place, I ran after her to the edge of the ravine; but I arrived too late even to apologize. All I saw of her was a scornful flick of her beautiful tail as she disappeared into the warren of crevices on the far side of the gully, driving her pups before her.

17

Visitors from Hidden Valley

ALTHOUGH I continued my vigil at the observation tent well into July, I did not add much to my knowledge of the wolves. Because the pups were growing rapidly and needed increasingly large quantities of food, George, Angeline and Albert were forced to devote most of their energy and time to hunting far afield. During the brief periods when they were at the den they spent most of their time sleeping, since finding food for the pups had become an exhausting business. Nevertheless, occasionally they were still able to surprise me.

One day the wolves killed a caribou close to home and this convenient food supply gave them an opportunity to take a holiday. They did not go hunting at all that night, but stayed near the den and rested.

The next morning dawned fine and warm, and a general air of contented lassitude seemed to overcome all three. Angeline lay at her ease on the rocks overlooking the summer den, while George and Albert rested in sandy beds on the esker ridge. The only signs of life from any of them through the long morning were occasional changes of position, and lazy looks about the countryside.

Toward noon, Albert roused himself and meandered down to the bay to get a drink. Then for an hour or two he hunted sculpins in a desultory fashion, after which he started back toward his bed.

When he was halfway there he had to stop to relieve himself—an effort which seemed to exhaust him so thoroughly that he gave up the idea of going back to the crest of the esker and sprawled out where he was instead. His head instantly began to droop, and he was soon asleep.

He had not been unobserved. George had been lying with his head on his forepaws, casually watching the progress of his friend's fishing expedition. When Albert collapsed in sleep, George got up. He stretched, yawned hugely, and with an appearance of idle insouciance began to amble off toward the spot where Albert lay. He seemed quite aimless, stopping to sniff at shrubs and mouseholes, and twice sitting down to scratch himself. Nevertheless, he never lost sight of Albert—and when he had drifted to within fifty feet of the sleeping wolf his demeanor changed dramatically.

Lowering himself into an almost catlike crouch he began to inch toward Albert with every appearance of serious intent. The tension began to build, and I found myself clutching the telescope as I waited for the denouement, wondering what had prompted George's swift transformation. Had the perfect harmony of the family broken down at last? Had Albert somehow transgressed the wolfish code, and was he about to be made to pay for his transgressions with his blood? It looked that way.

With infinite caution, George slithered closer and closer to the unsuspecting sleeper. When he was ten feet from Albert—who was still dead to the world— George drew his hindquarters up under him and, after pausing long enough to fully savor the moment, launched himself in a tremendous leap while at the same time letting loose a terrifying roar.

The impact of a hundred and fifty odd pounds of pouncing wolf ought to have knocked the wind clean out of Albert; but he had some breath left—for he

produced a brand-new sound for my catalogue of wolf
noises. It was a high-pitched snarl of shock and outrage—not entirely unlike the sound I have heard an
angry woman make when, in a crowded subway car,
someone pinched her bottom.

George leaped away, already running, while behind him Albert struggled to his feet.

The chase which followed appeared to be in deadly
earnest. George shot up the slope of the esker as if
the hounds of hell were after him, while Albert
followed with a grim and furious determination. The
two of them jinked and dodged back and forth,
exerting themselves to the limits of their strength.

As they swept past the summer den, Angeline
bobbed up, took a quick look, and enthusiastically
joined in the chase. The odds were now two-to-one
against George, and he could no longer dodge but
was forced to rely on a straightaway flight which
carried him down off the esker, across the muskeg
below it, and along the shore of the bay.

There was a huge split rock on the shore near the
head of the bay, and George shot through the narrow interstice, swerved so abruptly that sand and
stones flew from under his feet, then circled sharply
back around the rock just in time to catch Angeline
broadside-on. He did not hesitate, but crashed deliberately into her, bowling her completely over and
sending her slithering on her side for half a dozen
feet.

One of his pursuers was now out of action temporarily, but George had lost his lead. Before he could
be off again, Albert was upon him and they went
down together, locked in combat. Meanwhile Angeline picked herself up and joined the fray.

The melee ended as suddenly as it had begun, and
the three wolves separated, shook themselves, sniffed
noses, wagged their tails hard, and trotted back
toward the den with every indication that a good
time had been had by all.

Practical jokes such as this were rare amongst the wolves, although I several times saw Angeline set an ambush for George when she spotted him at a distance returning from a hunting trip. On these occasions she would go into hiding and when he was almost abreast of her she would spring out at him. He always appeared to be startled; but this may have been assumed emotion, for in most cases his sense of smell must have warned him of her proximity. Once the surprise was over, Angeline would nuzzle her mate, embrace him with her forepaws, fling herself down in front of him with her hindquarters elevated, or skitter along beside him, bumping him affectionately with her shoulders. The whole thing seemed to be in the nature of a private little ritual of welcome.

Another event which took place during the July doldrums gave me much to think about. Although Angeline now frequently went hunting with the males, there were nights when she did not go, and during one of these she had visitors.

It was well after midnight and I was dozing in my tent when a wolf howled from somewhere south of me, and not too far away. It was an unusual call, rather muted, and with no quavers. Sleepily I picked up my binoculars and tried to locate the source. Eventually I found two wolves, both strangers, sitting on a point of land on my side of the bay and directly opposite to the wolf esker.

This discovery brought me fully awake, for I had come to assume that the territory of each wolf family was sacrosanct as far as other wolves were concerned. I knew Angeline was at home, for I had seen her entering the gully a little while earlier, and I was intensely curious to see how she would react to this intrusion.

When I trained my glasses on the gully (the telescope was not as good as ordinary binoculars for night viewing, in the twilight conditions which then prevailed) she had already emerged and was standing facing the point where the strangers were. She was keenly alert, with head thrust forward, ears cocked, and her tail stretched out astern like that of a setter.

None of the wolves moved or made a further sound for several minutes; then one of the strangers again essayed the rather tentative howl which I had already heard. Angeline reacted at once. She began slowly wagging her tail, and her tense attitude relaxed visibly. Then she trotted forward to the edge of the ravine and barked sharply.

Now I am aware that, according to the books, wolves (and Husky dogs) are not supposed to bark; but Angeline's bark was a bark and nothing else, and as soon as they heard it, the two strange wolves got to their feet and began trotting around the shore of the bay.

Angeline met them about a quarter of a mile from the den. Standing stock-still, she waited for them to approach, and when they were five or ten yards from her they too stopped. I could hear nothing; but the tails of all three wolves began to wave slowly back and forth, and after a minute or so of this mutal indication of good feeling, Angeline stepped gingerly forward and sniffed noses.

Whoever the strangers were, they were evidently welcome. When the greeting ceremonies had been concluded all three wolves trotted toward the summer den. At the edge of the ravine one of the strangers began to romp with Angeline, and these two played for several minutes, although far more gently than Angeline played with George, or George with Albert.

While this was going on the second stranger calmly descended into the depths of the ravine where the four pups were.

Unfortunately I could not see what took place in the ravine itself; but it was certainly nothing to disturb Angeline, for, having finished playing with her friend, she also walked to the edge of the ravine and stood there looking down, her tail wagging harder than ever.

The strangers did not stay long. After twenty minutes the one in the ravine re-emerged; there was further nose smelling among all three wolves, and then the strangers turned away and set off back the way they had come. Angeline accompanied them for some distance, frolicking first with one and then the other of them. It was not until they swung away from the shore of the bay and headed west that she turned for home.

When I told Ootek of what I had seen he was not at all surprised, although he seemed to find *my* surprise rather inexplicable. After all, he pointed out, people do visit other people; so what was odd about wolves visiting other wolves?

He had me there.

At this juncture Mike entered the discussion by asking me to describe the strange wolves. I did my best, and he nodded.

"I guess they come from the bunch in Hidden Valley," he said. "It is maybe three, four miles south of here. I see them many times. Two bitches and one dog wolf, and some pups. I guess one of them's the mother of the bitch you call Angeline; the other's Angeline's sister maybe. Anyhow in fall they all join up with your bunch and go south together."

I considered this information in silence for a few minutes and then I asked:

"Since only one of those two bitches has a mate, the other must still be a spinster—which one would it be, do you think?"

Mike gave me a long and thoughtful stare.

"Listen," he said, "how soon you figure to leave this country and go home, eh? I guess you been here too damn' long already."

18

Family Life

IN MID-JULY I decided it was time to give up my role as a static observer and to begin seriously studying the hunting activities of wolves.

This decision was hastened by the accidental uncovering of my long-neglected Operation Order from under a pile of dirty socks which had been accumulating on top of it for several weeks. I had almost forgotten, not only about the Order, but about Ottawa itself; but as I again leafed through the minutely detailed sheaf of instructions I realized I had been guilty of a dereliction of duty.

The orders plainly stated that my first task should have been to conduct a census and general survey of wolves, followed by an intensive study of "wolf-caribou-predator-prey relationships." Studies of the nature and the social behavior of wolves were thus placed firmly outside the frame of reference of my work, and so one morning I struck my little tent, packed up the telescope, and closed down my observation post. The following day Ootek and I loaded a camping outfit aboard the canoe, and set out on a prolonged cruise through the tundra plains to the northward.

We covered a good many hundreds of miles during the succeeding weeks, and gathered much information concerning wolf population and wolf-caribou-predator-prey relationships; together with a lot of associated information which, though it was unrelated to the Department's aims, could not be entirely ignored.

A semiofficial estimate of the wolf population of Keewatin had already been made by the competent authorities on the basis of information received from the usual trapper-trader sources, and the given figure was thirty thousand wolves. Even with my sketchy grasp of mathematics I was able to work this out as an average of one wolf to every six square miles. If one then took into account the fact that about a third of the tundra plains lay under water, while another third consisted of barren rock hills and ridges where neither caribou, wolf nor most other beasts could make a living, the density rose to one wolf for every two square miles, approximately.

This seemed pretty dense. Indeed, had it been true, Ootek and I might have had trouble making progress due to the sheer pressure of wolves.

Unhappily for the theoreticians we found the wolves widely scattered, in the usual family groups —each family occupying a territory of one to three hundred square miles, although this dispersal was by no means uniform. We located one site, for instance, where two families had denned within half-a-mile of each other; and Ootek told me he had once found three females, each with a litter of pups, denning within a few feet of one another on an esker near the Kazan River. On the other hand, we traveled for three days through what looked like good wolf country on the Thlewiaza River and never saw a footing, a scat, or a hair of a wolf. Reluctantly, and recognizing that it was not going to endear me to my employers, I was forced to revise the population estimate downward to three thousand, and at that I was probably guilty of gross exaggeration.

The families we encountered were of all sizes from a single pair of adults with three pups to a group of seven adults and ten pups. Since, in every case but one, there were extra adults, and since I could learn nothing about their relative status in the family except by murdering them (which would have enabled me only to determine age and sex), I again resorted to Ootek for information.

Female wolves do not breed until they are two years old, and males not until they are three, he told me. Until they are of breeding age most of the adolescents remain with their parents; but even when they are of age to start a family they are often prevented from doing so by a shortage of homesteads. There is simply not enough hunting territory available to provide the wherewithal for every bitch to raise a litter. Since an overpopulation of wolves above the carrying capacity of the country to maintain would mean a rapid decline in the numbers of prey animals—with consequent starvation for the wolves themselves—they are forced to practice what amounts to birth control through continence. Some adult wolves may have to remain celibate for years before a territory becomes available. However, because the period of urgent amorous appetite is short —only about three weeks out of the year—these bachelors and spinsters probably do not suffer any great feeling of sexual deprivation. Moreover, their desire for domesticity and the companionship of other adults, as well as pups, is apparently met by the communal nature of the family group. Indeed, Ootek believed some wolves actually preferred the "uncle" or "aunt" status, since it gave them the pleasures of being involved in rearing a family without incurring the full responsibilities of parenthood.

Old wolves, particularly those who had lost their mates, also tended to remain celibate. Ootek told me of a wolf he had encountered every year for sixteen years who, during the first six years of this period, fathered an annual litter. During the seventh winter his mate disappeared, possibly poisoned by bounty hunters in the south. The following spring he was back at his old den. But although a litter of pups was reared there that season, they belonged to another pair of wolves; perhaps, so Ootek thought, to the widower's son and daughter-in-law. In any event the old wolf remained supernumerary to the establishment for the rest of his life, although continuing to share in the task of providing for the pups.

Apart from the fact that there are only a fixed number of homesteads available to the wolves, their abundance is apparently further restricted by a built-in birth-control mechanism. Thus it happens that when food species are abundant (or the wolf population is scanty) bitches give birth to large litters—sometimes of as many as eight pups. But if the wolves are too numerous, or food is scarce, the number of pups in a litter may fall to as few as one or two. This is also true of other arctic animals, such as rough-legged hawks. In a year when the small mammal population is high, roughlegs will lay five or six eggs in a clutch; but when mice and lemmings are scarce, they may lay a single egg or they may not breed at all.

Epidemic disease is the overriding factor which ensures that, even if other controlling factors fail to operate, the wolf population will not become too large for the capacity of the prey animals to maintain it. On those rare occasions when the general balance is upset (often as a result of man's interference) and wolves become too abundant, they soon begin to weaken physically as food grows scarce and malnutrition grades into outright starvation. At times such as these devastating epidemics of rabies, distemper or mange invariably appear among the wolves, and their numbers are quickly reduced to a bare survival level.

In 1946 the lemmings (which in the Canadian arctic are a cyclic species whose peak of abundance occurs every four years followed by a population drop to near the zero mark) were at the low point in their cycle. Coincidentally, the drastically depleted caribou herds of Keewatin* chose that year to alter their

*The Canadian caribou population has dropped from about 4,000,000 in 1930 to less than 170,000 animals in 1963.

age-old migration habits, and most of them by-passed southern central Keewatin entirely. It was a disastrous season for the Eskimos, foxes and wolves alike. Hunger lay heavy on the land. The latent rabies virus flared up among the starving foxes, and the wolves began to contract the disease too.

Now, animals stricken with rabies do not "go mad" in the usual sense of the word. Their nervous systems are affected so that they become erratic and unpredictable, and they lose the protection of a sense of fear. Rabid wolves sometimes walk blindly into speeding automobiles and trains; they have come stumbling in among entire teams of Huskies and have been torn to pieces as a result; and not infrequently they have wandered into village streets and have even entered tents or houses occupied by men. Such wolves, sick to the verge of death, are pitiable objects; but the human reaction to them is usually one of unbridled terror—not of the disease, for it is seldom recognized as rabies, but of the wolves themselves. Grotesque incidents occur which help to sustain the general myth about the vicious and dangerous nature of the wolf.

One such sick and dying wolf appeared in Churchill during the 1946 epidemic. It was first encountered by a Canadian Army corporal wending his way back to barracks after a session at the Churchill beer hall. According to the corporal's account, a gigantic wolf leaped at him with murderous intent, and he barely escaped with his life by running a mile to the shelter of the guardhouse. He could exhibit no physical evidence of his ordeal, but his psychic scars were evidently deep. His warning sent the whole Army camp into a panic of near-hysterical proportions. American and Canadian contingents alike were mobilized, and squads of grim-faced men armed with rifles, carbines and spotlights were soon scouring the surrounding country intent on dealing with a menace which, in a matter of hours, had grown into several packs of starving wolves.

During the ensuing excitement eleven Husky dogs, one American Pfc, and a Chippewayan Indian coming home late became casualties—not of the wolf, but of the vigilantes.

For two days children and women stayed indoors. Foot soldiers all but vanished from the Army camp, and men on missions to distant buildings either went by jeep, well armed, or did not go at all.

A wolf was glimpsed on the second day by a light Army aircraft which had joined the hunt, and an intrepid detachment of Mounted Police sallied forth to deal with it. The wolf turned out to be a cocker spaniel belonging to the Hudson's Bay Company manager.

Not until the third day did the panic ease. Late that afternoon the driver of a six-ton Army truck, returning to the camp from the airport, suddenly saw a bundle of fur on the road ahead of him. He jammed on the brakes but was unable to stop in time, and the wolf—by then so sick it could no longer move—was mercifully killed.

The aftermath was interesting. To this day there are residents of Churchill (and no doubt also a number of soldiers scattered over the continent) who will, at the drop of a hat, describe the invasion of Churchill by wolves in 1946. They will tell you of desperate personal encounters; of women and children savaged; of dog teams torn to ribbons; and of an entire human community living in a state of siege. All that is lacking is the final dramatic description of the North American equivalent of a Russian troika fleeing across the frozen plains, inevitably to be overwhelmed by a wave of wolves, while the polar night resounds to the crunching sound of human bones being cracked by wolfish jaws.

19

Naked to the Wolves

THE WEEKS which we spent cruising the tundra plains were idyllic. The weather was generally good, and the sensation of freedom which we derived from the limitless land was as invigorating as the wide-ranging life we led.

When we found ourselves in the territory of a new wolf family we would make camp and explore the surrounding plains for as long as was required in order to make the acquaintance of the group. We were never lonely, despite the immensity and solitude of the country, for the caribou were always with us. Together with their attendant flocks of herring gulls and ravens, they imparted a sense of animation to what might otherwise have seemed a stark enough landscape.

This country belonged to the deer, the wolves, the birds and the smaller beasts. We two were no more than casual and insignificant intruders. Man had never dominated the Barrens. Even the Eskimos, whose territory it had once been, had lived in harmony with it. Now these inland Eskimos had all but vanished. The little group of forty souls to which Ootek belonged was the last of the inland people, and they were all but swallowed up in this immensity of wilderness.

We encountered other human beings only on a single occasion. One morning, shortly after starting on our journey, we rounded a bend in a river and Ootek suddenly raised his paddle and gave a shout.

On the foreshore ahead of us was a squat skin tent. At the sound of Ootek's cry, two men, a woman and three half-grown boys piled out of the tent and ran to the water's edge to watch us approach.

We landed and Ootek introduced me to one of the families of his tribe. All that afternoon we sat about drinking tea, gossiping, laughing and singing, and eating mountains of boiled caribou meat. When we turned in for the night Ootek told me that the men of the family had pitched their camp at this spot so they could be in position to intercept the caribou who crossed the river at a narrows a few miles farther downstream. Paddling one-man kayaks and armed with short stabbing spears, these men hoped to be able to kill enough fat animals at the crossing to last them through the winter. Ootek was anxious to join in their hunt, and he hoped I would not mind remaining here for a few days so that he could help his friends.

I had no objection, and the next morning the three Eskimo men departed, leaving me to bask in a magnificent August day.

The fly season was over. It was hot and there was no wind. I decided to take advantage of the weather to have a swim and get some sun on my pallid skin, so I went off a few hundred yards from the Eskimo camp (modesty is the last of the civilized vices which a man sheds in the wilds), stripped, swam, and then climbed a nearby ridge and lay down to sun-bathe.

Wolflike, I occasionally raised my head and glanced around me, and about noon I saw a group of wolves crossing the crest of the next ridge to the north.

There were three wolves, one of them white, but the other two were almost black—a rare color phase. All were adults, but one of the black ones was smaller and lighter than the rest, and was probably a female.

I was in a quandary. My clothes lay by the shore some distance away and I had only my rubber shoes and my binoculars with me on the ridge. If I went back for my clothes, I knew I might lose track of these wolves. But, I thought, who needed clothes on a day like this? The wolves had by now disappeared over the next crest, so I seized my binoculars and hared off in pursuit.

The countryside was a maze of low ridges separated by small valleys which were carpeted with grassy swales where small groups of caribou slowly grazed their way southward. It was an ideal terrain for me, since I was able to keep watch from the crests while the wolves crossed each of these valleys in turn. When they dropped from view beyond a ridge I had only to sprint after them, with no danger of being seen, until I reached another elevated position from which I could watch them traverse the succeeding valley.

Sweating with excitement and exertion I breasted the first ridge to the north, expecting to see some frenzied action as the three wolves came suddenly down upon the unsuspecting caribou below. But I was disconcerted to find myself looking out over a completely peaceful scene. There were about fifty bucks in view, scattered in groups of three to ten animals, and all were busy grazing. The wolves were sauntering across the valley as if they had no more interest in the deer than in the rocks. The caribou, on their part, seemed quite unaware of any threat. Three familiar dogs crossing a farm pasture would have produced as much of a reaction in a herd of domestic cattle as the wolves did among these caribou.

The scene was all wrong. Here was a band of wolves surrounded by numbers of deer; but although each species was obviously fully aware of the presence of the other, neither seemed perturbed, or even greatly interested.

Incredulously, I watched the three wolves trot by within fifty yards of a pair of young bucks who were lying down chewing their cuds. The bucks turned their heads to watch the wolves go by, but they did not rise to their feet, nor did their jaws stop working. Their disdain for the wolves seemed monumental.

The two wolves passed on between two small herds of grazing deer, ignoring them and being ignored in their turn. My bewilderment increased when, as the wolves swung up a slope and disappeared over the next crest, I jumped up to follow and the two bucks who had been so apathetic in the presence of the wolves leaped to their feet, staring at me in wild-eyed astonishment. As I sprinted past them they thrust their heads forward, snorted unbelievingly, then spun on their heels and went galloping off as if pursued by devils. It seemed completely unjust that they should have been so terrified of *me*, while remaining so blasé about the wolves. However, I solaced myself with the thought that their panic might have resulted from unfamiliarity with the spectacle of a white man, slightly pink, and clad only in boots and binoculars, racing madly across the landscape.

I nearly ran right into the wolves over the next crest. They had assembled in a little group on the forward slope and were having a social interlude, with much nose smelling and tail wagging. I flung myself down behind some rocks and waited. After a few moments the white wolf started off again and the others followed. They were in no hurry, and there was considerable individual meandering as they went down the slopes toward the valley floor where scores of deer were grazing. Several times one or another of the wolves stopped to smell a clump of moss, or detoured to one side to investigate something on his own. When they reached the valley they were strung out in line abreast and about a hundred feet apart, and in this formation they turned and trotted along the valley floor.

Only those deer immediately in front of the wolves showed any particular reaction. When a wolf approached to within fifty or sixty yards, the deer would snort, rise on their hind feet and then spring off to one side of the line of advance. After galloping a few yards some of them swung around again to watch with mild interest as the wolf went past, but most returned to their grazing without giving the wolf another glance.

Within the space of an hour the wolves and I had covered three or four miles and had passed within close range of perhaps four hundred caribou. In every case the reaction of the deer had been of a piece—no interest while the wolves remained at a reasonable distance; casual interest if the wolves came very close; and avoiding-tactics only when a collision seemed imminent. There had been no stampeding and no panic.

Up to this time most of the deer we had encountered had been bucks; but now we began to meet numbers of does and fawns, and the behavior of the wolves underwent a change.

One of them flushed a lone fawn from a hiding place in a willow clump. The fawn leaped into view not twenty feet ahead of the wolf, who paused to watch it for an instant, then raced off in pursuit. My heart began to thud with excitement as I anticipated seeing a kill at last.

It was not to be. The wolf ran hard for fifty yards without gaining perceptibly on the fawn, then suddenly broke off the chase and trotted back to rejoin his fellows.

I could hardly believe my eyes. That fawn should have been doomed, and it certainly would have been if even a tenth of the wolfish reputation was in fact deserved; yet during the next hour at least twelve separate rushes were made by all three wolves against single fawns, a doe with a fawn, or groups of does and fawns, *and in every case the chase was broken off almost before it was well begun.*

I was becoming thoroughly exasperated. I had not

run six miles across country and exhausted myself just to watch a pack of wolves playing the fool.

When the wolves left the next valley and wandered over the far crest, I went charging after them with blood in my eye. I'm not sure what I had in mind— possibly I may have intended to chase down a caribou fawn myself, just to show those incompetent beasts how it was done. In any event I shot over the crest—and straight into the middle of the band.

They had probably halted for a breather, and I burst in among them like a bomb. The group exploded. Wolves went tearing off at top speed in all directions—ears back, tails stretching straight behind them. They ran scared, and as they fled through the dispersed caribou herds the deer finally reacted, and the stampede of frightened animals which I had been expecting to witness all that afternoon became something of a reality. Only, and I realized the fact with bitterness, it was not the wolves who had been responsible—it was I.

I gave it up then, and turned for home. When I was still some miles from camp I saw several figures running toward me and I recognized them as the Eskimo woman and her three youngsters. They seemed to be fearfully distrait about something. They were all screaming, and the woman was waving a two-foot-long snowknife while her three offspring were brandishing deer spears and skinning knives.

I stopped in some perplexity. For the first time I became uncomfortably aware of my condition. Not only was I unarmed, but I was stark naked. I was in no condition to ward off an attack—and one seemed imminent, although I had not the slightest idea what had roused the Eskimos to such a mad endeavor. Discretion seemed the better part of valor, so I stretched my weary muscles and sprinted hard to bypass the Eskimos. I succeeded, but they were still game, and the chase continued most of the way back to the camp where I scrambled into my trousers, seized my rifle, and prepared to sell my life dearly. Fortunately Ootek and the men arrived back at the camp just as the woman and her crew of furies swept down upon me, and battle was averted.

Somewhat later, when things had quieted down, Ootek explained the situation. One of the children had been picking berries when he had seen me go galloping naked across the hills after the wolves. Round-eyed with wonder, he had hastened back to report this phenomenon to his mother. She, brave soul, assumed that I had gone out of my mind (Eskimos believe that no white man has very far to go in this direction), and was attempting to assault a pack of wolves bare-handed and bare everything else. Calling up the rest of her brood, and snatching what weapons were at hand, she had set out at top speed to rescue me.

During the remainder of our stay, this good woman treated me with such a wary mixture of solicitude and distrust that I was relieved beyond measure to say farewell to her. Nor was I much amused by Ootek's comment as we swept down the river and passed out of sight of the little camp.

"Too bad," he said gravely, "that you take off your pants. I think she like you better if you left them on."

20

The Worm i' the Bud

I QUERIED Ootek about the apparently inexplicable behavior of the band of wolves I had seen at the Eskimo camp, and in his patient and kindly fashion he once more endeavored to put me straight.

To begin with, he told me that a healthy adult caribou can outrun a wolf with ease, and even a three-week-old fawn can outrun all but the swiftest wolf. The caribou were perfectly well aware of this, and therefore knew they had little to fear from wolves in the normal course of events. The wolves were fully aware of it too, and, being highly intelligent, they seldom even attempted to run down a healthy caribou—knowing full well that this would be a senseless waste of effort.

What the wolves did instead, according to Ootek, was to adopt a technique of systematically testing the state of health and general condition of the deer in an effort to find one which was not up to par. When caribou were abundant this testing was accomplished by rushing each band and putting it to flight for just long enough to expose the presence, or absence, of a sick, wounded or otherwise inferior beast. If such a one was revealed, the wolves closed on it and attempted to make a kill. If there was no such beast in the herd, the wolves soon desisted from the chase and went off to test another group.

When caribou were hard to find, different techniques were used. Several wolves acting in concert would sometimes drive a small herd of deer into an

ambush where other wolves were waiting; or if caribou were very scarce, the wolves might use a relay
system whereby one wolf would drive the deer towards another wolf posted some distance away, who
would then take up the chase in his turn. Techniques
such as these decreased the caribou's natural advan-
tages, of course, but it was usually still the weakest
or at any rate the least able deer which fell victim
to the pursuing wolves.

"It is as I told you," Ootek said. "The caribou feeds
the wolf, but it is the wolf who keeps the caribou
strong. We know that if it were not for the wolf
there would soon be no caribou at all, for they would
die as weakness spread among them."

Ootek also stressed the fact that, once a kill had
been made, the wolves did no more hunting until the
supply of food was completely gone and they were
forced by hunger to go back to work.

These were novel concepts to one who had been
taught to believe that wolves were not only capable
of catching almost anything but, actuated by an insatiable blood lust, would slaughter everything which
came within their range.

Of the hunts I subsequently watched, almost all
followed the pattern of the first one I had seen. The
hunters, numbering from one to as many as eight
individual wolves, would be observed trotting un-
hurriedly through the dispersed groups of deer, who
almost invariably seemed quite unconcerned by the
presence of their "mortal enemies." Every now and
again a wolf, or sometimes two or three, would turn
aside from the line of march and make a short dash
at some nearby deer, who would wait until the
attackers were about a hundred yards distant before
throwing up their heads and galloping off disdain-
fully. The wolves would stop and watch the deer
go. If they ran well and were obviously in good fettle,
the wolves would then turn away.

The testing was not haphazard and I began to see

a pattern of selection emerging. It was very seldom indeed that wolves bothered testing the herds of prime bucks, who were then at the peak of condition, having done nothing all summer but eat and sleep. It was not that these bucks were dangerous adversaries (their great spreads of antlers are useless as weapons) but simply that the wolves did not stand a chance of closing with them, and they knew it.

Mixed herds of does with fawns were much more interesting to the wolves, for the percentage of injured, malformed or inferior individuals is naturally higher among the fawns, who have not yet been subjected to any prolonged period of rigorous natural selection.

Groups of aged and sterile does were also a favorite target for testing. Sometimes one of these old and weakened beasts would be concealed in the midst of a herd of prime and vigorous animals; but the wolves, who must have known the caribou almost as intimately as they knew themselves, would invariably spot such a beast and test what looked to my eyes like a hopelessly healthy and active herd.

Fawns were often tested more severely than adults, and a wolf might chase a fawn for two or three hundred yards; but unless the young animal had given signs of weakness or exhaustion within that distance, the chase was usually abandoned.

Economy of effort seemed to be a guiding principle with the wolves—and an eminently sensible one too, for the testing process often had to be continued for many hours before the wolves encountered a caribou sufficiently infirm to be captured.

When the testing finally produced such a beast, the hunt would take a new turn. The attacking wolf would recklessly expend the energy he had been conserving during the long search, and would go for his prey in a glorious surge of speed and power which, if he was lucky, would bring him close behind the fleeing deer. Panic-stricken at last, the deer would begin frantically zigzagging—a foolish thing to do, I thought, since this enabled the wolf to take short cuts and close the gap more quickly.

Contrary to one more tenet of the wolf myth, I never saw a wolf attempt to hamstring a deer. Drawing upon all his strength, the wolf would forge up alongside the caribou and leap for its shoulder. The impact was usually enough to send the deer off balance and, before it could recover, the wolf would seize it by the back of the neck and bring it down, taking care to avoid the wildly thrashing hoofs, a blow from any one of which could cave in the wolf's ribcage like so much brittle candy.

The kill was quickly, and usually cleanly, made and I doubt very much if the deer suffered any more than a hog suffers when it is being butchered for human consumption.

The wolf never kills for fun, which is probably one of the main differences distinguishing him from man. It is hard work for a wolf to catch and kill a big game animal. He may hunt all night and cover fifty or sixty miles of country before he is successful —if he *is* successful even then. This is his business, his job, and once he has obtained enough meat for his own and his family's needs he prefers to spend the rest of his time resting, being sociable, or playing.

Contrary to yet another misconception, I know of no valid evidence that wolves kill more than they can use, even when the rare opportunity to do so arises. A kill made during the denning season is revisted time and again until the last ounce of meat has been stripped from it. Often—if gulls, ravens, foxes and other scavengers are numerous—the wolf will dismember the carcass and bury sections of it at considerable distances from the site of the kill in order to preserve it for his own use. Later in the season, when the united family is freely roaming its territory, the band will camp near each kill until it is completely consumed.

Of sixty-seven wolf-killed caribou which I examined after the wolves were finished with them, few consisted of anything except bones, ligaments, hair and offal. In most cases even the long-bones had been cracked for the marrow content; and in some cases the skull had been gnawed open—a formidable task even for a wolf.

Another point of interest is that what little remained of most of these carcasses showed evidence of disease or serious debility. Bone deformations, particularly those caused by necrosis of the skull, were common; and the worn state of the teeth of many skulls showed that these belonged to old and enfeebled animals. Fresh kills, where the whole carcass was available for examination, were hard to come by; but on a number of occasions I reached a deer almost as soon as the wolves had killed it and, with inexcusable gall, shooed the wolves away. They went timidly enough, albeit unhappily. Several of these deer were so heavily infested with external and internal parasites that they were little better than walking menageries, doomed to die soon in any case.

As the weeks wore on toward the summer's end, the validity of Ootek's thesis became more and more obvious. The vital importance played by the wolf in preserving rather than in destroying the caribou seemed irrefutable to me, although I was by no means sure it would appear in the same light to my employers. I needed overwhelming proof if I was to convince them, and preferably proof of a solidly material nature.

With this in mind, I began making collections of the parasites found in wolf-killed caribou. As usual, Ootek took a keen interest in this new aspect of my work; but it was a short-lived interest.

Through all of recorded time his people had been

caribou eaters, living largely on raw or only partly
cooked meat, because of the shortage of fuel for fires.
Ootek himself was weaned on caribou meat,
pre-chewed for him by his mother, and it had been
his staple food ever since he gave up mother's milk.
Consequently he took his meat for granted, and it
had never occurred to him to turn an analytical eye
upon his daily bread. When he saw me producing
scores of varieties and thousands of individual worms
and cysts from various parts of caribou anatomy, he
was greatly surprised.

One morning he was watching in somber fascination as I dissected a particularly pest-ridden old buck.
I always tried to explain what I was doing so that
he would understand the nature of my studies, and
this seemed to be as good a time as any to brief him
on the subject of parasitization. Hauling a bladder
cyst about the size of a golfball out of the caribou's
liver, I explained that this was the inactive form of a
tapeworm, and that, if eaten by a carnivore, it would
eventually develop into several segmented creatures
about thirty feet in length, coiled neatly in the new
host's intestines.

Ootek looked sick.

"You mean when it is eaten by a wolf?" he asked
hopefully.

"*Nahk*," I replied, exercising my growing Eskimo
vocabulary. "Foxes, wolves, even people will do. It
will grow in any of them, though perhaps not as well
in people."

Ootek shuddered and began to scratch his stomach as if conscious of an itching sensation in that
region.

"I do not like liver, fortunately," he said, greatly
relieved now that he had remembered this fact.

"Oh, these worms are found all through the caribou," I explained, with the enthusiasm of an expert
enlightening a layman. "Look here. See these spots in
the rump meat? White men call this 'measled meat.'"

These are the resting forms of another kind of worm. I do not know for sure if it will grow in people. But these—" and here I deftly extracted some thread-like nematode worms, each ten or more inches in length, from the dissected lungs—"these have been found in men: in fact enough of them will choke a man to death in a very little while."

Ootek coughed convulsively and his mahogany-dark face grew wan again.

"That is enough," he pleaded when he had got his breath back. "Tell me no more! I go now, back to the camp, and there I will think hard of many things and I will forget what you have told me. You are not kind. For if these things be true, then surely I will have to eat fish like an otter, or else starve to death. But perhaps this is a white man's joke?"

There was such a pathetic note of hope in his question that it roused me from my professor's trance and I belatedly realized what I was doing to the man.

I laughed, if in a somewhat artificial manner.

"*Eema*, Ootek. It is a joke on you. Only a joke. Now go you back to camp and cook our supper of big steaks. Only," and in spite of myself I could not restrain the adjuration, "make damn' sure you cook them well!"

21

School Days

By MID-SEPTEMBER the tundra plains burned somberly in the subdued glow of russet and umber where the early frosts had touched the ground cover of low shrubbery. The muskeg pastures about Wolf House Bay were fretted with fresh roads made by the southbound herds of caribou, and the pattern of the wolves' lives had changed again.

The pups had left the summer den and, though they could not keep up with Angeline and the two males on prolonged hunts, they could and did go along on shorter expeditions. They had begun to explore their world, and those autumnal months must have been among the happiest of their lives.

When Ootek and I returned to Wolf House Bay after our travels through the central plains, we found that our wolf family was ranging widely through its territory and spending the days wherever the hunt might take it.

Within the limits imposed upon me by my physical abilities and human needs, I tried to share that wandering life, and I too enjoyed it immensely. The flies were all gone. Though there were sometimes frosts at night, the days were usually warm under a clear sun.

On one such warm and sunlit day I made my way north from the den esker, along the crest of a range of hills which overlooked a great valley, rich in forage, and much used by the caribou as a highway south.

A soot-flecking of black specks hung in the pallid sky above the valley—flocks of ravens following the deer herds. Families of ptarmigan cackled at me from clumps of dwarf shrub. Flocks of Old Squaw ducks, almost ready to be off for distant places, swirled in the tundra ponds.

Below me in the valley rolled a sluggish stream of caribou, herd after herd grazing toward the south, unconscious, yet directly driven by a knowledge that was old before we even knew what knowledge was.

Some miles from the den esker I found a niche at the top of a high cliff overlooking the valley, and here I settled myself in comfort, my back against the rough but sun-warmed rock, my knees drawn up under my chin, and my binoculars leveled at the living stream below me.

I was hoping to see the wolves and they did not disappoint me. Shortly before noon two of them came into sight on the crest of a transverse ridge some distance to the north. A few moments later two more adults and the four pups appeared. There was some frisking, much nose smelling and tail wagging, and then most of the wolves lay down and took their ease, while the others sat idly watching the caribou streaming by on either side only a few hundred feet away.

I easily recognized Angeline and George. One of the other two adults looked like Uncle Albert; but the fourth, a rangy dark-gray beast, was a total stranger to me. I never did learn who he was or where he came from, but for the rest of the time I was in the country he remained a member of the band.

Of all the wolves, indeed of all the animals in view including the caribou and myself, only George seemed to feel any desire to be active. While the rest of us sprawled blissfully in the sun, or grazed lethargically amongst the lichens, George began to wander restlessly back and forth along the top of the ridge. Once or twice he stopped in front of An-

geline but she paid him no attention other than to
flop her tail lazily a few times.

Drowsily I watched a doe caribou grazing her way
up the ridge on which the wolves were resting. She
had evidently found a rich patch of lichens and,
though she must have seen the wolves, she continued
to graze toward them until not twenty yards
separated her from one of the pups. This pup
watched her carefully until, to my delight, he got to
his feet, stared uneasily over his shoulder to see what
the rest of the family was doing, then turned and slunk
toward them with his tail actually between his legs.

Not even the restless George, who now came slowly
toward the doe, his nose outthrust as he tasted her
scent, seemed to disturb her equanimity until the
big male wolf, perhaps hurt in his dignity by her
unconcern, made a quick feint in her direction. At
that she flung her head high, spun on her ungainly
legs and gallumphed back down the ridge apparently
more indignant than afraid.

Time slipped past, the river of deer continued to
flow, and I expected to observe nothing more exciting
than this brief interlude between the doe and the
wolves, for I guessed that the wolves had already
fed, and that this was the usual after-dinner siesta.
I was wrong, for George had something on his mind.

A third time he went over to Angeline, who was
now stretched out on her side, and this time he would
not take "no" for an answer. I have no idea what he
said, but it must have been pertinent, for she
scrambled to her feet, shook herself, and bounced
amiably after him as he went to sniff at the slumber-
ing forms of Uncle Albert and the Stranger. They
too got the message and rose to their feet. The pups,
never slow to join in something new, also roused and
galloped over to join their elders. Standing in a rough
circle, the whole group of wolves now raised their
muzzles and began to howl, exactly as they used to do
at the den esker before starting on a hunt.

I was surprised that they should be preparing for a hunt so early in the day, but I was more surprised by the lack of reaction to the wolf chorus on the part of the caribou. Hardly a deer within hearing even bothered to lift its head, and those few who did contented themselves with a brief, incurious look toward the ridge before returning to their placid grazing. I had no time to ponder the matter, for Angeline, Albert and the Stranger now started off, leaving the pups sitting disconsolately in a row on the crest, with George standing just ahead of them. When one of the youngsters made an attempt to follow the three adults, George turned on him, and the pup hurriedly rejoined his brothers and sisters.

What little wind there was blew from the south and the three wolves moved off upwind in a tight little group. As they reached the level tundra they broke into a trot, following one another in line, not hurrying, but trotting easily through the groups of caribou. As usual the deer were not alarmed and none took evasive action except when the wolves happened to be on a collision course with them.

The three wolves paid no attention to the caribou either, although they passed many small herds containing numbers of fawns. They made no test runs at any of these groups, but continued purposefully on their way until they were almost abreast the niche where I was sitting. At this point Angeline stopped and sat down while the other two joined her. There was more nose smelling, then Angeline got up and turned toward the ridge where George and the pups still sat.

There were at least two hundred deer between the two groups of wolves, and more were coming constantly into view around the eastern shoulder of the transverse ridge. Angeline's glance seemed to take them all in before she and her companions began to move off. Spreading out to form a line abreast, with intervals of a couple of hundred yards between them so that they almost spanned the whole width of the valley, they now began to run north.

They were not running hard, but there was a new purposefulness to their movements which the deer seemed to recognize; or perhaps it was just that the formation the wolves were using made it difficult for the herds to avoid them in the usual way by running off to one side. In any event herd after herd also began to turn about and move north, until most of the caribou in the valley were being driven back the way they had come.

The deer were clearly reluctant to be driven, and several herds made determined efforts to buck the line; but on each occasion the two nearest wolves converged toward the recalcitrant caribou and forced them to continue north. However, three wolves could not sweep the whole width of the valley; the deer soon began to discover that they could swing around the open wings and so resume their southerly progress. Nevertheless, by the time the wolves were nearing the ridge, they were herding at least a hundred deer ahead of them.

Now for the first time the deer showed real signs of nervousness. What had become an almost solid mass of a hundred or more animals broke up into its constituent small bands again, and each went galloping off on its own course. Group after group began to swerve aside, but the wolves no longer attempted to prevent them. As the wolves galloped past each of these small herds, the caribou stopped and turned to watch for a moment before resuming their interrupted journey south.

I was beginning to see what the wolves were up to. They were now concentrating their efforts on one band of a dozen does and seven fawns, and every attempt which this little herd made to turn either left or right was promptly foiled. The deer gave up after a while, and settled down to outrun their pursuers in the straightaway.

They would have done it, too, but as they swept past the clump of willows at the end of the ridge a perfect flood of wolves seemed to take them in the flank.

I could not follow events as well as I would have wished because of the distance, but I saw George racing toward a doe accompanied by two fawns. Then, just as he reached them, I saw him swerve away. He was passed by two pups going like gray bullets. These two went for the nearest of the two fawns, which promptly began jinking. One of the pups, attempting too sharp a turn, missed his footing and tumbled head over heels, but he was up on the instant and away again.

The other pups seemed to have become intermingled with the balance of the deer, and I could not see what they were up to; but as the herd drew away at full gallop the pups appeared in the rear, running hard, but losing ground.

A single fawn now began outdistancing its pursuers too. All four pups were still running flat out, although they no longer had a chance of overtaking any of the deer.

What of the adult wolves meanwhile? When I swung my glasses back to look for them I found George standing exactly where I had seen him last, his tail wagging slowly as he watched the progress of the chase. The other three wolves had by now returned to the crest of the ridge. Albert and the Stranger had lain down to rest, after their brief exertions, but Angeline was standing up and watching the rapidly retreating caribou.

It was half an hour before the pups came back. They were so weary they could hardly climb the ridge to join their elders, all of whom were now lying down relaxing. The pups joined the group and flopped, panting heavily; but none of the adults paid them any heed.

School was over for the day.

22

Scatology

As SEPTEMBER slipped into October and the white nights hardened the muskegs and skimmed the lakes with ice, I would have been glad to spend all my time afield, living the life of a pseudo-wolf to the fullest. However, I did not have the freedom of the wolves. An immense backlog of scientific trivia awaited my attention at the cabin. On the theory (my own, and not my employers) that my time should be spent observing living wolves, I had deliberately neglected the innumerable peripheral studies which had been ordained for me by Ottawa. Now, as the time grew short, I felt I should at least make a gesture of compliance to authority.

One of the sideshows with which I had been saddled was a vegetation study. It consisted of three parts: first I had to make a collection of all the species of plants in the area; then I had to make a "cover degree" study, to determine the ratios of various plants one to the other; and finally I was expected to do a "content analysis," to determine the nutritional value of the vegetation from the point of view of the caribou.

There was no time left to do all these things so I compromised by tackling the "cover degree" study.

This involved the use of a Raunkiaer's Circle, a device designed in hell. In appearance it was all simple innocence, being no more than a big metal hoop; but in use it was a devil's mechanism for driving sane men mad. To use it, one stood on a stretch of muskeg, shut one's eyes, spun around several times like a top, and then flung the circle as far away as possible. This complicated procedure was designed to ensure that the throw was truly "random"; but, in the event, it inevitably resulted in my losing sight of the hoop entirely, and having to spend an unconscionable time searching for the thing.

Once the hoop was found, misery began in earnest. I was then expected to pluck every plant, no matter how minute, which lay within its charmed circle; identify and count the number of species; and then count *individuals* belonging to each species.

It sounds easy? It is not. Barren Land plants are small in any case, and many of them are almost microscopic. My first attempt with the circle cost me the best part of a day, gave me severe eyestrain, and resulted in a seizure in the lumbar region as a result of spending too many hours crouched like a demented rabbit over the circle, while plucking plantlets with a pair of tweezers.

I had discouraged Ootek from accompanying me on my Raunkiaer expeditions, since I simply did not feel capable of explaining what it was all about. However, during my third day of torture he appeared over a nearby ridge and bore happily down upon me. My greeting was a little sour, for the milk of human kindness was not flowing in my veins. Painfully standing erect I picked up the circle and made my next throw, while he watched with interest.

The circle did not go very far, for I was weary and discouraged, and there was no strength in me.

"*Shweeanak!* Pretty poor," Ootek commented disparagingly.

"Dammit!" I cried hotly. "Let's see you do better!"

I think my guardian angel must have inspired that challenge. Ootek grinned in a superior sort of manner, ran over to the circle, picked it up, swung back his arm like a discus thrower, and let fly. The circle rose like a fleeing partridge, glittered brilliantly in the sunshine as it reached the top of its trajectory, sailed gracefully out over a nearby tundra pond and, with barely a splash, sliced into the water and disappeared forever.

Ootek was stricken with remorse. His face tightened with apprehension as he waited for my anger to explode. I suppose he never understood why I threw my arms about him and led him gaily through several steps of an Indian jig before taking him back to the cabin and splitting my last, precious bottle of wolf-juice with him. But the incident no doubt confirmed his conviction that the ways of the white man are indeed inscrutable.

With the plant study so fortuitously ended, I was faced with another distasteful duty—the completion of my scatalogical studies.

Because of the importance attached to scatology in Ottawa, I had been ordered to devote part of my time to collecting and analyzing wolf scats. This was not a task with which I was enraptured, but as I went about the Barrens I had kept a casual eye open for scats. Using a long pair of forceps I had collected those I found and placed them in small canvas bags, each of which bore a label indicating the approximate age of the specimen and where and when it was collected. I kept these little bags under my bunk in the cabin, and by the end of September I had amassed such a formidable collection that there was not room for them all and they had begun to spill out on the floor and get underfoot.

For a variety of reasons, not least of which was the mental image I had formed of Ootek's and Mike's expressions when they realized what I was doing, I was loath to begin analyzing my finds. I had managed to keep my scat-collecting activities secret, and although Mike and Ootek may have been curious about the contents of my little bags they were too polite (or too fearful of what they might be told) to question me on the subject. Even though they had both become reasonably tolerant of the idiosyncrasies involved in my professional duties, I did not want to try them too far and so I continued to postpone the analytical work, until one October morning when they went away together on a caribou hunting trip, leaving me in sole possession of the camp. Feeling reasonably assured of privacy I then prepared to come to grips with my unpleasant task.

Due to the effect of weathering, followed by prolonged storage, the scats had become as hard as rocks and had to be softened before I could work on them. I therefore carted them down to the riverbank and put them to soak in two galvanized pails filled with water. While the softening process was taking place I laid out my tools, notebooks and other equipment on a large flat rock exposed to the sun and to a steady breeze. I felt the task ahead of me was one which could best be conducted in an unconstrained environment.

The next step was to don my gas mask. I am not trying to be funny when I record this fact. I had been supplied with the gas mask, along with a case of tear-gas grenades with which I was supposed to drive wolves out of their dens so they could be shot as autopsy specimens. Naturally I would never have stooped so low, even before I came to know and respect the wolves as friends. I had long since dumped the bombs into the nearby lake; but I had retained the mask, since I was charged with it. It now became useful, because wolf scats sometimes carry the eggs of a particularly baneful parasite which, if inhaled by man, hatch into minute worms that bore their way into his brain where they encyst, frequently with fatal results both to themselves and to their host.

Having ascertained that the first batch of scats was

in a pliable condition, I donned the mask, placed a scat on a white enamel plate which I had borrowed from the cabin, and began dissecting it with forceps and scalpel. As I identified its constituents through a hand lens, I noted the information in my record book.

It was a laborious process, but not devoid of interest. In fact I soon became so wrapped up in my work that I ceased to be aware of my surroundings.

Consequently when I stood up an hour or two later to stretch my muscles, and casually turned toward the cabin, I was intensely surprised to find myself confronted by a semicircle of a dozen unfamiliar Eskimos who were staring at me with expressions of incredulity mingled with revulsion.

It was a disconcerting moment. I was so startled that I forgot about the gas mask, with its elephantine snout and goggle eyes; and when I tried to greet these strangers my voice, filtered through two inches of charcoal and a foot of rubber pipe, had the muffled and lugubrious quality of wind blowing through a tomb—an effect which filled the Eskimos with consternation.

Hastily attempting to redeem myself I tore off the mask and stepped briskly forward—whereupon the Eskimos, with the precision of a musical comedy chorus line, stepped briskly backwards, staring at me the while with wild surmise.

Desperate to show my good intentions, I smiled as broadly as I could, thereby baring my teeth in what must have seemed a fiendish grin. My visitors responded by retreating another yard or two, and some of them shifted their gaze apprehensively to the shining scalpel clutched in my right hand.

They were clearly poised for flight; but I saved what was left of the situation by recalling appropriate Innuit words and blurting out a more or less formal welcome. After a long pause one of them ventured a timid reply, and gradually they ceased to eye me like a flock of chickens in the presence of a rattle-snake.

Although there was no real rapport between us, the stilted conversation which followed revealed that these people formed a part of Ootek's band which had spent the summer farther east and had only just returned to the home camps, where they had been told of the presence of a strange white man at Mike's cabin. They had thereupon decided to come and see this phenomenon for themselves; but nothing they had heard in advance had prepared them for the spectacle which met their eyes when they arrived.

As we talked I noticed several children and some of the adults casting surreptitious glances at the scat pails and at the enamel plate with its litter of hair and mouse bones. In any other people this would have represented simple curiosity, but I had now spent enough time with Eskimos to appreciate the obliquity of their minds. I interpreted their interest as a subtle suggestion that they were hungry and thirsty after their long journey and would appreciate some tea and food.

Since in Mike's absence I was the host, and since hospitality is the greatest of virtues in the North, I invited the Eskimos to join me in the cabin for a meal that evening. They seemed to understand and to accept my offer and, leaving me to complete my work on the last few scats, they withdrew to a nearby ridge to pitch their travel camp.

The results of the analysis were most interesting. Some 48 per cent of the scats contained rodent remains, largely incisor teeth and fur. The balance of the identifiable food items included fragments of caribou bones, caribou hair, a few bird feathers and, surprisingly, a brass button much corroded by the action of digestive juices but still bearing a recognizable anchor-and-cable motif such as is used in various merchant navy services. I have no idea how this but-

ton happened to end up where it did, but its presence
cannot be taken as evidence of a wolf having eaten
some wandering sailor.*

Watched by two solemn little Eskimo boys, I now
washed out the pails, then filled them with fresh
water with which to make the several gallons of tea
I knew would be required. As I walked back to the
cabin I noted that the little boys were haring it up
the ridge as if filled with great tidings which they
were anxious to impart to their elders, and I smiled
at their enthusiasm.

My cheerful mood did not survive for long. Three
hours later dinner was ready (it consisted of fish
balls cooked Polynesian style with a sweet-and-sour
sauce of my own devising), and there was no sign of
my guests. It was already dark, and I began to worry
lest there had been some misunderstanding about the
time of dinner.

Eventually I put on my parka, took a flashlight, and
went in search of the Eskimos.

I never found them. Indeed, I never saw them
again. Their camp site was abandoned, and the people had vanished as totally as if the great plains had
swallowed them down.

I was much puzzled, and somewhat offended.
When Ootek returned the next day I told him the
story and demanded an explanation. He asked a number of searching questions about pails, scats, and
other things—questions which did not seem to me
to be particularly relevant. And in the end, he failed
me—for the first time in our association. He insisted
that he could not possibly explain why my hospitality
had been so rudely spurned . . . and he never did.

---

*There is no authentic report of wolves ever having killed a
human being in the Canadian North; although there must have
been times when the temptation was well-nigh irresistible.

23

To Kill a Wolf

THE TIME was drawing near when I would have to leave Wolf House Bay—not because I wished to, but because the wolves would soon be departing to their wintering grounds.

During late October, when winter begins to savage the bleak plains, the caribou turn their backs on the tundra and begin working their way down into the alien but sheltered world of forests. And where they go, the wolves must follow; for in winter there is nothing left upon the frozen plains for the wolves to eat.

From early November until April the wolves and caribou travel together through the *taiga*, the sparse borderline forests of stunted spruce and jackpine lying below the timberline. In years when the snow-shoe rabbits are abundant, the wolves prey heavily upon them; but always they stay close to the deer —since, in time of famine, only deer can save them.

Each wolf family travels as a group, but it is not uncommon for two or three small groups to come together into a single band. There appear to be no fixed rules about this, and such a band can break up into its component parts again at any time. However, there are upper limits to the numbers in a given band. Winter hunting requires a close degree of co-operation between several wolves if the hunt is to be successful; but if there are too many wolves they will not all get enough to eat from a given kill. A band of from five to ten individuals seems to be about the ideal size.

They do not appear to have fixed territories in winter. Each band hunts where and as it pleases, and when two strange bands meet they have been observed to greet each other and then go their separate ways.

A concentration of bands seldom occurs in any one area. How they manage to keep dispersed, and thereby avoid the dangers of too many wolves and too little food, is not known; but the Chippewayan Indians say it is done by means of urine messages which are left on every prominent point, rock, or tree around the lakes and along the well-used trails. The fact remains that, unless outright starvation sweeps the land, the nomadic winter wolf bands, moving at the whim of the equally nomadic caribou herds, somehow manage to avoid treading on one another's toes.

For the Barren Land wolves winter is the time of death.

Once they have entered timber they are exposed to a concentrated, highly skilled, and furious assault from men. Trappers cannot bear them, for wolves not only compete for caribou but can wreak havoc with a trapline, springing the light traps used for foxes without getting caught themselves. Furthermore, most white trappers are afraid of wolves—some of them deathly afraid—and there is nothing like the whip of fear to lash men into a fury of destruction.

The war against wolves is kept at white heat by Provincial and Federal Governments, almost all of which offer wolf bounties ranging from ten dollars to thirty dollars per wolf; and in times when the value of foxes and other furs is depressed, this bounty becomes in effect a subsidy paid to trappers and traders alike.

Much is said and written about the number of deer reputedly slaughtered by wolves. Very little is said about the actual numbers of wolves slaughtered by men. In one case a general falsehood is widely and officially disseminated; in the other the truth seems to be suppressed. Yet one trapper operating along the boundary between Manitoba and Keewatin, in the winter of the first year of my study, collected bounty on a hundred and eighteen wolves of which one hundred and seven were young ones born the previous spring. According to law he should have killed those wolves by trapping or shooting them. In fact he did what everyone else was doing—and still does in the Far North, with the covert permission of Governments: he spread strychnine so indiscriminately over an immense area that almost the entire population of foxes, wolverines and many lesser flesh-eaters was wiped out. That did not matter since foxes fetched no price that year. Wolves were worth twenty dollars each for bounty.

Traps and poison are the commonest wolf-killers; but there are other methods in wide use as well. One is the airplane, a favorite of those civic-minded sportsmen who serve society by sacrificing their time and money to the destruction of vermin. The crew of a high-flying aircraft keeps watch for wolves in the open, preferably on the ice of a lake. When one is found the aircraft is flown low over him and the beast is pursued so long and hard that he frequently collapses and sometimes dies even before a blast of buckshot strikes him.

However, I know of one occasion when this method failed of its purpose. Two men in their own light aircraft had flown out from a large city to help rid the world of wolves. During previous hunts they had killed many, and the pilot had become adept at chasing the beasts so closely that his skis would almost strike them. One day he came too close. The harassed wolf turned, leaped high into the air, and snapped at one of the skis. He died in the ensuing crash; but so did the two men. The incident was described in an article in a widely distributed sportsman's magazine as an example of the cunning and dangerous nature of the wolf, and of the boundless courage of the men who match themselves against him. This is, of course, a classic gambit. Whenever and wherever men have engaged in the mindless slaughter of animals (including other men), they have often attempted to justify their acts by attributing the most vicious or revolting qualities to those they would destroy; and the less reason there is for the slaughter, the greater the campaign of vilification.

Antiwolf feelings at Brochet (the northern Manitoba base for my winter studies) when I arrived there from Wolf House Bay were strong and bitter. As the local game warden aggrievedly described the situation to me: the local people had been able to kill 50,000 caribou each winter as recently as two decades past, whereas now they were lucky if they could kill a couple of thousand. Caribou were becoming scarce to the point of rarity, and wolves were unanimously held to be to blame. My rather meek remonstrance to the effect that wolves had been preying on caribou, without decimating the herds, for some tens of thousands of years before the white men came to Brochet, either fell on deaf ears or roused my listeners to fury at my partisanship.

One day early in the winter a trader burst into my cabin in a state of great excitement.

"Listen," he said challengingly, "you've been screaming for proof wolves butcher the herds. Well, hitch up your team and get out to Fishduck Lake. You'll get your proof! One of my trappers come in an hour ago and he seen fifty deer down on the ice, all of 'em killed by wolves—and hardly a mouthful of the meat been touched!"

Accompanied by a Cree Indian companion I did

as I was bid, and late that afternoon we reached
Fishduck Lake. We found a sickening scene of
slaughter. Scattered on the ice were the carcasses of
twenty-three caribou, and there was enough blood
about to turn great patches of snow into crimson slush.

The trapper had been correct in stating that no
use had been made of the carcasses. Apart from some
minor scavenging by foxes, jays and ravens, all but
three of the animals were untouched. Two of those
three were bucks—minus their heads; while the
third, a young and pregnant doe, was minus both
hindquarters.

Unfortunately for the "proof," none of these deer
could have been attacked by wolves. There were no
wolf tracks anywhere on the lake. But there were
other tracks: the unmistakable triple trail left by the
skis and tail-skid of a plane which had taxied all over
the place, leaving the snow surface scarred with a
crisscross mesh of serpentine lines.

These deer had not been pulled down by wolves,
they had been shot—some of them several times.
One had run a hundred yards with its intestines
dragging on the ice as a result of a gut wound. Several of the others had two or more bullet-broken limbs.

The explanation of what had actually happened
was not far to seek.

Two years earlier, the tourist bureau of the Provincial Government concerned had decided that Barren Land caribou would make an irresistible bait
with which to lure rich trophy hunters up from the
United States.* Accordingly a scheme was developed
for the provision of fully organized "safaris" in which
parties of sportsmen would be flown into the subarctic, sometimes in Government-owned planes, and,
for a thousand dollars each, would be guaranteed a
first-rate set of caribou antlers.

---

*In 1963 the Newfoundland Government is using the same
gambit.

During the winter sojourn of the caribou inside the timberline they feed in the woods at dawn and dusk and spend the daylight hours yarded on the ice of the open lakes. The pilot of the safari aircraft, therefore, had only to choose a lake with a large band of caribou on it and, by circling for a while at low altitude, bunch all the deer into one tight and milling mob. Then the aircraft landed; but kept under way, taxiing around and around the panic-stricken herd to prevent it from breaking up. Through open doors and windows of the aircraft the hunters could maintain a steady fire until they had killed enough deer to ensure a number of good trophies from which the finest might be selected. They presumably felt that, since the jaunt was costing a great deal of money, they were entitled to make quite certain of results; and it is to be assumed that the Government officials concerned agreed with them.

When the shooting was over the carcasses were examined and the best available head taken by each hunter, whose permit entitled him to "the possession of" only a single caribou. If the hunters were also fond of venison a few quarters would be cut off and thrown aboard the plane, which would then depart southward. Two days later the sports would be home again, victorious.

The Cree who accompanied me had observed this sequence of events for himself the previous winter while acting as a guide. He did not like it; but he knew enough of the status of the Indian in the white man's world to realize he might just as well keep his indignation to himself.

I was more naïve. The next day I radioed a full report of the incident to the proper authorities. I received no reply—unless the fact that the Provincial Government raised the bounty on wolves to twenty dollars some weeks afterwards could be considered a reply.

24

The World We Lost

THE PROBLEM of how I was to make my way south to Brochet from Wolf House Bay was resolved one morning when Ootek burst into the cabin to announce that he had seen an aircraft. Sure enough, a Norseman plane on floats was lazily circling over the tundra to the west of us.

I had long since given up hope that the pilot who had brought me to Wolf House Bay would ever return, and so the sight of this plane sent me into a dither of excitement. Remembering the smoke generators with which I had been supplied, I ran to get them. To my surprise they worked. A mighty coil of black and oily smoke went soaring into the high skies and the Norseman (which had disappeared to the west) reappeared, homing on my signal column.

It landed in the bay, and I went out by canoe to greet the pilot, a narrow-faced and unprepossessing-looking young man chewing a wad of gum. He had much to tell me.

As the months had passed without any word from me, my Department had grown increasingly disturbed. Not only had they received no wolf reports, but some four thousand dollars' worth of Government equipment had vanished into the tundra void. This was serious, since some inquisitive member of the Opposition might at any time have got wind of the matter and asked a question in the House of Commons. The possibility of being accused of carelessness in the handling of the public funds is a bogy which haunts every Government department.

The Royal Canadian Mounted Police were therefore asked to find me, but clues were scarce. The pilot who had taken me into the Barrens had since gone missing on a flight over the Mackenzie district and the police couldn't find any trace of *him*, let alone discover what he had done with me. Eventually, and after a great deal of sleuthing, the police got hold of the rumor circulating in Churchill to the effect that I was a Secret Service agent who had been sent to spy on the floating Russian bases at the pole, and they so reported to Ottawa, adding that they did not like being made mock of, and the next time the Department wanted something found, it had better be honest with them.

The pilot who had landed to investigate my smoke signal had not been sent to look for me but was engaged in a prospecting survey, and his discovery of me was purely fortuitous. However, he agreed to carry a message back to his base informing the Department where its equipment was, and suggesting that a plane be sent to pick it up immediately, before the freeze-up came.

With Mike's assistance the pilot took advantage of the landing to top up his gas tanks from drums carried in the fuselage. Meanwhile I departed to complete some unfinished business at the wolf-den esker.

In order to round out my study of wolf family life, I needed to know what the den was like inside—how deep it was, the diameter of the passage, the presence (if any) of a nest at the end of the burrow, and such related information. For obvious reasons I had not been able to make this investigation while the den was occupied, and since that time I had been too busy with other work to get around to it. Now, with time running out, I was in a hurry.

I trotted across-country toward the den and I was

within half-a-mile of it when there was a thunderous roar behind me. It was so loud and unexpected that I involuntarily flung myself down on the moss. The Norseman came over at about fifty feet. As it roared past, the plane waggled its wings gaily in salute, then lifted to skim the crest of the wolf esker, sending a blast of sand down the slope with its propeller wash. I picked myself up and quieted my thumping heart, thinking black thoughts about the humorist in the now rapidly vanishing aircraft.

The den ridge was, as I had expected (and as the Norseman would have made quite certain in any case), wolfless. Reaching the entrance to the burrow I shed my heavy trousers, tunic and sweater, and taking a flashlight (whose batteries were very nearly dead) and measuring-tape from my pack, I began the difficult task of wiggling down the entrance tunnel.

The flashlight was so dim it cast only an orange glow—barely sufficient to enable me to read the marks on the measuring-tape. I squirmed onward, descending at a forty-five-degree angle, for about eight feet. My mouth and eyes were soon full of sand and I was beginning to suffer from claustrophobia, for the tunnel was just big enough to admit me.

At the eight-foot mark the tunnel took a sharp upward bend and swung to the left. I pointed the torch in the new direction and pressed the switch.

Four green lights in the murk ahead reflected back the dim torch beam.

In this case green was not my signal to advance. I froze where I was, while my startled brain tried to digest the information that at least two wolves were with me in the den.

Despite my close familiarity with the wolf family, this was the kind of situation where irrational but deeply ingrained prejudices completely overmaster reason and experience. To be honest, I was so frightened that paralysis gripped me. I had no weapon of any sort, and in my awkward posture I could barely have gotten one hand free with which to ward off an attack. It seemed inevitable that the wolves *would* attack me, for even a gopher will make a fierce defense when he is cornered in his den.

The wolves did not even growl.

Save for the two faintly glowing pairs of eyes, they might not have been there at all.

The paralysis began to ease and, though it was a cold day, sweat broke out all over my body. In a fit of blind bravado, I shoved the torch forward as far as my arm would reach.

It gave just sufficient light for me to recognize Angeline and one of the pups. They were scrunched hard against the back wall of the den; and they were as motionless as death.

The shock was wearing off by this time, and the instinct for self-preservation was regaining command. As quickly as I could I began wiggling back up the slanting tunnel, tense with the expectation that at any instant the wolves would charge. But by the time I reached the entrance and had scrambled well clear of it, I had still not heard nor seen the slightest sign of movement from the wolves.

I sat down on a stone and shakily lit a cigarette, becoming aware as I did so that I was no longer frightened. Instead an irrational rage possessed me. If I had had my rifle I believe I might have reacted in brute fury and tried to kill both wolves.

The cigarette burned down, and a wind began to blow out of the somber northern skies. I began to shiver again; this time from cold instead of rage. My anger was passing and I was limp in the aftermath. Mine had been the fury of resentment born of fear: resentment against the beasts who had engendered naked terror in me and who, by so doing, had intolerably affronted my human ego.

I was appalled at the realization of how easily I had forgotten, and how readily I had denied, all that the summer sojourn with the wolves had taught me about them . . . and about myself. I thought of Angeline and her pup cowering at the bottom of the den where they had taken refuge from the thundering apparition of the aircraft, and I was shamed.

Somewhere to the eastward a wolf howled; lightly, questioningly. I knew the voice, for I had heard it many times before. It was George, sounding the wasteland for an echo from the missing members of his family. But for me it was a voice which spoke of the lost world which once was ours before we chose the alien role; a world which I had glimpsed and almost entered . . . only to be excluded, at the end, by my own self.

Epilogue

During the winter of 1958–1959 the Canadian Wildlife Service, in pursuance of its continuing policy of
wolf control, employed several Predator Control
officers to patrol the Keewatin Barrens in ski-equipped
aircraft for the purpose of setting out poison bait
stations.

In early May of 1959, one of these officers landed
at Wolf House Bay. He remained in the vicinity for
some hours and placed a number of cyanide "wolf
getters" in appropriate places near the den, which,
so he ascertained, was occupied. He also spread a
number of strychnine-treated baits in the vicinity.

He was unable to return at a later date to check on
this control station, because of the early onset of the
spring thaws.

It is not known what results were obtained.

ABOUT THE AUTHOR

For nearly thirty years FARLEY MOWAT has written of the lands, seas and peoples of the Far North with a humor and raciness, an understanding and compassion that place him internationally among Canada's most distinguished authors.

Born in Belleville, Ontario in 1921, Mowat grew up in Belleville, Trenton, Windsor, Saskatoon, Toronto and Richmond Hill as his librarian father moved a household that included a miniature menagerie around the country; those early adventures were chronicled in *Owls in the Family* and *The Dog Who Wouldn't Be*. During World War II Mowat served in the army, entering as a private and emerging with the rank of captain. The experience of battle seared the imagination of the young soldier and ultimately gave rise to his most recent book, *And No Birds Sang*, a gripping eyewitness account of combat in Italy and Sicily.

Following his discharge, Mowat renewed his interest in the Canadian Arctic, an area he had first visited as a young man with an ornithologist uncle. Since 1949 he has lived in or visited almost every part of Canada and many other lands, including the distant regions of Siberia. He has said of himself, "I am a Northern Man . . . I like to think I am a reincarnation of the Norse saga men and, like them, my chief concern is with the tales of men, and other animals, living under conditions of natural adversity." His experiences have inspired such works as *People of the Deer*, *The Desperate People*, *Never Cry Wolf*, *A Whale for the Killing* and *The Boat Who Wouldn't Float*. Farley Mowat's twenty-five books have been published in over twenty languages in more than forty countries.

BANTAM
SHOP-AT-HOME
C·A·T·A·L·O·G

Special Offer
Buy a Bantam Book
for only 50¢.

*Now you can have Bantam's catalog filled with hun-
dreds of titles plus take advantage of our unique and
exciting bonus book offer. A special offer which gives
you the opportunity to purchase a Bantam book for
only 50¢. Here's how!*

*By ordering any five books at the regular price per
order, you can also choose any other single book
listed (up to a $4.95 value) for just 50¢. Some restric-
tions do apply, but for further details why not send
for Bantam's catalog of titles today!*

*Just send us your name and address and we will
send you a catalog!*